When I first met Terri Savelle Foy, I wondered what this beautiful, petite woman with the "Minnie Mouse" voice would have to say. I loved seeing a woman emerge who is powerful yet humble, sweet yet passionate about God's Word, and dynamic in connecting with her audience. I believe this book will be a turning point for many hurting people . . . and that it will propel them into the place God has destined for them to reach.

DR. WENDY TREAT

Co-pastor of Christian Faith Center
Seattle, Washington

MAKE YOUR DREAMS BIGGER THAN YOUR MEMORIES

Don't Let Your Past Keep You From Your Future

TERRI SAVELLE FOY

Regal

From Gospel Light
Ventura, California, U.S.A.

Published by Regal
From Gospel Light
Ventura, California, U.S.A.
www.regalbooks.com
Printed in the U.S.A.

Scripture quotations are taken from the following:

AKJV—The American King James Version. Produced by Stone Engelbrite. Used by permission.
AMP—Scripture taken from THE AMPLIFIED BIBLE, Old Testament copyright © 1965, 1987
by the Zondervan Corporation. The Amplified New Testament copyright © 1958, 1987
by The Lockman Foundation. Used by permission.
CEV—Contemporary English Version. Copyright © American Bible Society, 1995.
ESV—Scripture taken from the *English Standard Version,* Copyright © 2001. The *ESV* and
English Standard Version are trademarks of Good News Publishers.
GOD'S WORD—Scripture taken from *GOD'S WORD. GOD'S WORD* is a copyrighted work of
God's Word to the Nations. Quotations are used by permission. Copyright 1995
by God's Word to the Nations. All rights reserved.
KJV—King James Version. Authorized King James Version.
THE MESSAGE—Scripture taken from *THE MESSAGE.* Copyright © by Eugene H. Peterson, 1993,
1994, 1995. Used by permission of NavPress Publishing Group.
NASB—Scripture taken from the *New American Standard Bible,* © 1960, 1962, 1963, 1968, 1971,
1972, 1973, 1975, 1977, 1995 by The Lockman Foundation. Used by permission.
NCV—Scriptures quoted from *The Holy Bible, New Century Version,* copyright Ó 1987, 1988, 1991
by Word Publishing, Nashville, Tennessee. Used by permission.
NIV—Scripture taken from the *Holy Bible, New International Version®.* Copyright © 1973, 1978,
1984 by International Bible Society. Used by permission of Zondervan Publishing House.
All rights reserved.
NKJV—Scripture taken from the *New King James Version.* Copyright © 1979, 1980, 1982
by Thomas Nelson, Inc. Used by permission. All rights reserved.
NLT—Scripture quotations marked *NLT* are taken from the *Holy Bible, New Living Translation,*
copyright © 1996. Used by permission of Tyndale House Publishers, Inc., Wheaton, Illinois 60189.
All rights reserved.
Psalms Now—Created by Leslie F. Brandt. Published by Concordia Publishing House,
3558 S. Jefferson, St. Louis, MO 63118, © 2004.
TEV—Scripture quotations are from *Today's English Version.* Copyright © American Bible Society
1966, 1971, 1976. Used by permission.
TLB—Scripture quotations marked (*TLB*) are taken from *The Living Bible,* copyright © 1971.
Used by permission of Tyndale House Publishers, Inc., Wheaton, IL 60189. All rights reserved.

Literary Agent Representation: Esther Fedorkevich, Fedd & Company, (615) 579-8161,
esther@feddandcompany.com.

Library of Congress Cataloging-in-Publication Data
Foy, Terri Savelle.
Make your dreams bigger than your memories / Terri Savelle Foy.
p. cm.
ISBN 978-0-8307-5471-7 (hardcover)
1. Christian life. 2. Regret—Religious aspects—Christianity. I. Title.
BV4909.F69 2010
248.8'6—dc22
2010002458

Rights for publishing this book outside the U.S.A. or in non-English languages are administered
by Gospel Light Worldwide, an international not-for-profit ministry. For additional information,
please visit www.glww.org, email info@glww.org, or write to
Gospel Light Worldwide, 1957 Eastman Avenue, Ventura, CA 93003, U.S.A.

To order copies of this book and other Regal products in bulk quantities,
please contact us at 1-800-446-7735.

*I want to dedicate this book to you—the person
who is reading it right now. I believe it is a divine appointment
for you to read this book from cover to cover in order
to give your past a burial . . . and to begin pursuing the
God-given dreams that are already on the inside of you.
Never again will your memories be bigger
than your dreams!*

CONTENTS

FOREWORD

The mountain is steep, and you've climbed long and hard to make it to the top. It's been your life-long dream to climb that mountain. You're almost there; every muscle in your body is screaming for rest, but you can't stop. You're too close to the top. Too close to realizing your dreams.

You keep pushing forward with everything within you when suddenly you feel someone grab your leg. You look down and see someone at your heels; there's a hand clenched to your leg, and you're being pulled down. You're frozen. You can't climb anymore, because you've changed your focus. You're looking down, not up. You quickly glance to the top and see that someone is there with a hand outstretched. All you have to do is reach up and take that hand. But you feel the pull at your heels, so you look back.

How many people are stuck because they can't move forward for looking backward? Their dreams are just ahead, and God's hand is outstretched. All they have to do is stay focused on Him, stay focused on their goal, and move forward. But Satan is at their heels reminding them of every sin and every mistake, heaping condemnation on them. All the while Jesus is waiting with His hand outstretched.

Through the years I've heard countless stories of people making wrong choices that have caused endless pain and sorrow to them and others around them. I've even had many confide in me personally about issues in their life they were struggling with that weighed them down—marriages that were being ripped apart because of adultery; shame brought on by abuse; failure in some area of their life; the list goes on. I've seen some of them agonize with guilt because of sin in their past, while some have had a hard time forgiving themselves and moving forward even though God has forgiven them.

Terri Savelle Foy opens the window to her past and shares with us some of her most painful and shameful memories. Her no-holds-barred, I'm-not-going-to-smooth-this-over-because-I'm-a-well-known-preacher's-kid approach gives the reader a connection with her, and we are reminded once again that "all have sinned, and come short of the glory of God" (Rom. 3:23, *KJV*).

Terri struggled with guilt over her past for many years. God had a plan for her life, but she couldn't step into the fullness of that plan until she learned how to accept His forgiveness and forgive herself. What can we learn from Terri and her story?

Know that there is nothing in your past that God cannot forgive, and that if God can forgive you, then you can forgive yourself. Know that you can live your dreams if you choose to shake off the bondage of the past, get a clear vision of what God wants for your life, and then move in that direction.

Terri takes her testimony a step further and shares about the process that helped her on her journey toward complete healing from her past. These strategies are outlined in a practical way that can bring hope and healing to everyone who is struggling with issues that are keeping them from realizing their dreams.

You will be encouraged, inspired and motivated as you read Terri's book. Then release all of the negative aspects of your past so that you can live the abundant life that God intends for you to live.

Joni Lamb
Author, co-founder of the Daystar Television Network
and host of *Joni*

ACKNOWLEDGMENTS

First, I want to thank the Lord for loving me so much! Thank You, Jesus, for being the healer of the brokenhearted, for being my redeemer and for being the lifter of my head. What an honor it is to share Your Word with others and to encourage readers with what You've done in my life. Thank You for enabling me to dream.

Thank you to my sweet husband, Rodney, for not giving up on our marriage. You held on when I let go. It was tough at first, but God has helped us grow, learn from our mistakes and love each other more. Thank You for believing in me and in the call of God on my life. It means so much to me to have your support. And thank you for letting me use you (as funny examples) in my illustrations! I love you, Roddy.

Thank you to my precious daughter, Kassidi, for believing in her mom so much! Being my only child, you sure end up in a lot of messages. Thank you for being my traveling buddy, my shopping buddy, and for sitting through countless church services hearing the same stories over and over. You are so valuable to me. Thank you for loving God and loving your mom so much! *Je t'adore* . . . with all my heart.

How do I thank my parents, Jerry and Carolyn Savelle, for all they have done to teach me God's Word? Mom and Dad, you are living examples of the unconditional love of God. Thank you for raising me in a Christian home, for forgiving me for not making the best choices at times, and for always believing in me. You are the same behind the scenes as you are in front of people. Who would have thought that your little red-headed, freckle-faced Terra La Berra would be writing a book? Because of you, I have been given opportunities to share my message . . . and I do not take that lightly. I am so honored and so grateful to be your daughter.

Thank you to my sister, Jerri, for providing me with so many stories! We have so many funny childhood memories. I hope you don't mind me telling the world. We are opposite in so many ways, but we always have that "sister thing" that we share with no one else. All we have to do is look at each other and we know what the other person is thinking! I love you . . . and your six kids so much!

Thank you to my best friend, Theresa Paschall, for being bold enough to speak the truth to me . . . in love. It sure helps having a best friend who is also a counselor. I owe you thousands of dollars in therapy, Theresa! Thank you for being so trustworthy. You know everything there is to know about me . . . and you still love me and believe in me! That's a true best friend. I value your prayers, your opinions, your phone calls, your text messages and our weekly Mexican lunches . . . more than you know! Thank you for being my covenant friend for life.

Thank you to my assistant, Donna Groover, for keeping me on target with writing this book. You always have your little day planner reminding me of deadlines! Most of all, thank you for holding me accountable and loving me enough to speak the truth into my life. I appreciate your honesty . . . and your prayers. I am so thankful that God brought you from Jamaica to England to Texas to work with me.

Thank you, Isaiah Shook, for being a part of this ministry from the ground floor. You have done just about everything to help launch the ministry that God has put in my heart. From designing artwork to filming podcasts and from attending ladies' conferences to adding mascara (in photoshop) to some of my pale-looking pictures, you've done it all. Having your support and your God-given gifts on my team has brought such excellence to this ministry.

Thank you, Lucy Hinkle, for being my first partner in ministry! You have been encouraging me for years to write books, preach and practically run for president! Thank you for all the prayers, all the sweet cards on my desk and all the pep talks along the way. You were definitely used of the Lord to help me get started. I just have to say it: "I love Lucy."

Thank you, Esther Fedorkevich, for finding me. You are a wonderful literary agent who God used to encourage me to write this book! You saw potential in me even when I didn't realize it. Thank you for truly making this book happen. My sweet friend with the funny last name, you are a blessing to my life!

I would also like to say a great big thank you to my beautiful editor, A.J. Gregory. You have a way with words! Thank you for cleaning things up and making me sound so smart! You are anointed to write, and I thank you from my heart.

In closing, I want to thank the ministers who brought the Word of God to my life that changed me from the inside out:

Jerry Savelle (Dad), Joyce Meyer, Mac Hammond, Jesse Duplantis, Jeff Wickwire, (the late) Lester Sumrall, Stormie Omartian and Beth Moore. I played your CDs for hours and hours every day as I drove around, did laundry, cleaned house, walked, went to work and fell asleep. I am so thankful for your messages and your books, because they opened my eyes to the truth and prevented me from throwing away God's plan for my life. Your ministry birthed mine, and you will receive equal credit for every life that is blessed by this book. "How beautiful upon the mountains are the feet of him who brings good tidings, who publishes peace" (Isa. 52:7, *AMP*). Your feet will forever be beautiful in the Savelle-Foy household.

1

WHEN YOU LOOK BACK ...
YOU'VE LOST YOUR FUTURE

It was 5:30 in the morning when I was out walking in my neighborhood, getting some exercise. Filled with anxiety, I had little to no vision for my future. I was filled with enormous regret over my past. As I made my routine lap around the cul-de-sac, I was praying quietly under my breath. Begging God yet again to forgive me for my awful sins. But this time, something happened. I was struck with a vision.

I saw myself standing at the foot of the cross of Christ. When I looked up and saw Jesus' feet, blood was dripping from them onto the top of my head. In the depths of my heart, I clearly heard the Lord gently speak these words to me, "I'm washing the memories of the past away," as His blood covered my head. The blood continued to flow down my body, covering my heart, and I heard Him whisper again, "I am the Healer of the brokenhearted" (see Isa. 61:1). The precious flow proceeded to run all the way down to the bottom of my feet, and again, I vividly heard the Lord say, "The residue of sin is gone from you."

The next thing I saw was a big arm reaching down and handing me a clipboard. On it were the words "This is an assignment on your life." I was then handed a set of keys, and a voice boomed, "And here are the keys to the Kingdom of heaven to help you fulfill your assignment."

Wow! Needless to say, that vision changed the course of my life. But what exactly did it mean? I believe that God was telling me (1) I was truly forgiven for my past; (2) I had an assignment from God, a future and a purpose for being born; and (3) God had given me everything necessary to fulfill that assignment. All I had to do was believe that I was forgiven. Since having that vision, John 17:4 has become one of my favorite verses: "I glorified you on earth by completing down to the last detail what you assigned me to do" (*THE MESSAGE*).

That vision came at a time when I was absolutely consumed with shame and guilt over my past. Because I am a visual learner, I believe that God knew I had to "see" the blood of Jesus truly forgiving me. I had to "see" that God still had a plan for my life, even though I had made some big mistakes. And I had to "see" that God believes in me. I believe that by the time you finish this book, you, too, will *see* that for your own life.

Living in the past is deadly. It's designed to kill you. Kill your future. Kill your dreams. Kill your potential. Kill your confidence. Think about what your past means to you. It could represent anything from sexual abuse by a family member to a mistake you made just last night or a secret you have been hiding for 20 years.

What images run through your mind? Do thoughts of your past produce a negative emotional response? Do you *sigh* really big and think, *If people only knew* . . . ? Does it make you think of all the mistakes you've made or regrets you hang on to? Does the past bring a face to your mind that you want to get out of your mind? Does it make you feel anger, rage and deep feelings of rejection? Do you feel overwhelming regret, guilt and shame that you just can't seem to shake?

I don't know what the past means to you personally, but you do, and more importantly, God does. If you are truly fed up with being limited or even paralyzed by your past, and you simply want a new beginning, you're reading the right book.

For many years, I could not get past my past—past mistakes, past relationships, past hurts, past disappointments. I spent most of my prayer time praying over the past. I relived the past when I lay down at night, when I woke up in the morning and when I went about my day. I was letting my past define my future, and it was destroying any potential God gave me to do something with my life.

I am such a firm believer that you have a limited time on earth to do everything you possibly can with your life. God allowed you to be born for a purpose. So no matter what has happened in your past, God can still use you. He wants to use you. Do not die with your potential untapped because of something that happened back then! There's too much you've still got to do!

Remember Lot's Wife

It is recorded in Luke 17:32 that Jesus said, "Remember Lot's wife!" You may be familiar with the story of Lot's wife from Genesis 19. God was getting ready to destroy the city of Sodom and Gomorrah because the inhabitants were wicked and their lives were corroded with sin. God's heart was broken that all these people He created to love Him were doing nothing but looking for new ways to rebel against Him. God promised to save a man named Lot, and his family, from the destruction, and He gave them one command as they were on their way out: "Don't look back" (Gen. 19:17, *NIV*).

But what happened as they left? Lot's wife looked back and she was turned into a pillar of salt. I heard Joyce Meyer once say that when this woman turned back, she gave the impression that she cared more about her past than she did her future. Lot's wife lost her future by looking back. The reality is that you, too, can lose your future by looking back!

Sometimes I wonder what God had planned for Lot's wife to accomplish. What was on her clipboard? How do you suppose her story could have been written if she hadn't turned back? Would she have made a name for herself rather than be called "Lot's Wife"? Was her life so meaningless that nobody even remembered her name?

I hope this story alarms you. An alarm is meant to wake you up. I hope that statement (Don't look back!) wakes you up the way it woke me up in understanding how serious this is. Don't destroy your life by looking back. It's over. It's behind you. Everything about your past is finished! God wants to do a new thing in your life, but He can't do it if you keep lingering in your past.

"Regret" Is a Bad Word

I was walking out of my office gates one day, looking straight ahead, when suddenly I turned around. *Bam!* A car came out of nowhere and hit me on the right side. Instantly, I woke up from that startling dream, wondering what it was all about. It was so real. *We're not supposed to die in our dreams*, I thought. Next, I heard the Lord speak so clearly in my heart these life-changing words:

21

"If you continue to look back at the life I've delivered you from, your life will be summed up in one word: regret."

I don't know about you, but I don't want to come to the end of my life and have only regret. What are some regrets that may be plaguing you right now? What is causing you to keep looking back? What continues to catch your eye? What still possesses your heart? What is it in your life that you know is not God's best but it hurts too bad to let go of? What happened to you that has made you think you're not as good as other people?

I'm sure you know people who live in the past. Whenever you are around them, every conversation begins with the words "I remember when" and ends with "the past." They see themselves through their past experiences and believe that everyone else does as well. The truth is that nobody wants to hear it. It gets old, tiring and boring very quickly. In Philippians 3:13-14, Paul says, "One thing I do, forgetting those things which are behind and reaching forward to those things which are ahead, I press toward the goal for the prize of the upward call of God in Christ Jesus" (*NKJV*). In Matthew 12:34, Jesus also says, "Out of the abundance of the heart the mouth speaks" (*NKJV*). Apparently what happened to some people 10, 20 or 30 years ago is still in abundance in their heart, because it keeps coming out of their mouth.

If this is you, then you're reading the right book. It's time to let things be done with and behind you once and for all. Don't waste another day of your life allowing Satan to torment you over the past. Now, I'm not telling you to just get over it. Believe me, I know how frustrating hearing those words can be. And I know that just hearing them over and over didn't work for me. I needed more. I needed a strategy. And that's exactly what this book is: a step-by-step plan to lead you out of your past and into your vision and dreams.

Sin Happens to Us All

We all have a past. We've all made mistakes and done things we wish we hadn't done. We all wish we could just push a delete button on some of the choices we made yesterday and some of the things we've experienced, and then pretend they never happened. At least I do. Oh, how badly I do. You can't imagine how many times I have cried, "Why were you so stupid, Terri? Why? Why? Why did you do that? Why did you let that happen?" Or looked in the mirror and said, "I don't even know you. Wake up! What is wrong with you?"

Having grown up in church and listened to numerous testimonies of people who lived sinful lives, I knew that God is a forgiving God. However, the difference between the people giving those testimonies and me is that they weren't born again when they sinned. I was. They didn't know God, so who could blame them for all of their stumbles and messes? I, however, was a Christian all my life.

So why did I mess up so badly? What was my excuse? I didn't have one. Why was I flat-out sinning? I wasn't confused about God's commandments. I knew them very well. I just couldn't come to grips with how God could forgive *me*. I felt terrible for falling into Satan's traps, knowing full well the fact that the devil is my enemy.

The reason we, as Christians, fall into sin or disobey God is because we are deceived. Eve went through the same thing in the Garden. She knew God, and she knew exactly what God had said about the trees and the fruit. Eve wasn't confused. She even repeated God's instructions back to Him. She knew which tree, out of the whole Garden, was forbidden. So, why did she eat from the very tree that God specifically warned her about? She was deceived by Satan. He appealed to her flesh and preyed on her weakness. And he got her thinking. Anytime Satan can get you thinking about his suggestion, you can think yourself right out of the will of God for your life.

What happened right after Eve (and Adam) sinned? They immediately felt guilt, shame and regret. (I know these emotions all too well.) They felt unworthy to approach God and hid from Him in their fear. (Ah, exactly what Satan hoped for.) Let me tell you how I know about the guilt, shame and regret of wrong thinking and being taken in by Satan's deceptive ways.

What's Going On Behind the Smile?

I was a kid known for always smiling and being happy. But the girl who smiled a lot had a lot of pain behind that smile. I had been severely hurt by people in my young teenage years. I was manipulated, controlled, violated, abused, and painfully rejected. I felt insignificant. I may have seemed like a perfect child, but the truth is that I was a very insecure young girl who hid many painful things inside. The amazing part is not what I went through, but that I managed to hide it all behind a smile! I was very good at hiding my pain and keeping it all inside, which is a very dangerous thing.

I wanted so badly to please my parents and be perfect. I never wanted them to be worried about me messing up. So I turned into an overachiever. I made good grades and was in the National Honor Society program in high school. I was also homecoming queen; co-captain of the varsity cheerleaders; voted Miss Crowley High School; Class Favorite Girl; and I even dated the quarterback of the football team! I was blessed with many awards, was liked by most everybody, and stayed out of trouble. I *appeared* to have it all together, which was quite far from reality.

In college, it was no different. I was on the Dean's List nearly every semester. I loved God with all my heart. I prayed every night before I went to sleep. I got along with my roommates. Life was basically fun and carefree.

However, during the last semester of my senior year at Texas Tech University, this happy-go-lucky preacher's kid's life was torn apart. I found myself face down on my bedroom floor in an apartment in Lubbock, Texas, scribbling these words in my journal: "I want to die!" This seemingly "perfect Christian girl," who smiled all the time, was pregnant . . . before marriage.

It was a defining moment in my life. It was a moment that Satan was sure to take full advantage of . . . for as long as I would let him. I can't even articulate how overwhelmed I felt by shame, regret, guilt and hypocrisy. It seemed as if everything I had worked so hard for was for nothing. I was sure that my parents would cringe in seeing their perfect little girl become the biggest disgrace of our family.

I truly wanted to die.

I will never forget the day I found out that I was pregnant. I walked into a grocery store and nervously bought a home pregnancy test. I anxiously wondered if anyone from school would recognize me (knowing that I wasn't married) or, even worse, recognize me as Jerry Savelle's (the preacher's) daughter!

I was alone in my apartment when I took the test. My boyfriend waited on the other end of the telephone for the news. I furiously prayed and waited for the window on the stick to indicate a negative result. No such luck.

With my heart beating fast, and fear exploding in my body, I dropped the phone. On that August morning, a positive pink line confirmed my worst fears. I wasn't the good girl everyone thought. I couldn't hide my mistakes anymore. I hated myself.

Rather than tell my parents or admit to them that I really wasn't who they thought I was, I wanted to disappear or run away. I absolutely could not bear the pain of telling my folks. I knew I would embarrass them and their ministry and crush their hearts. I wanted to have the baby alone and never tell anyone what had happened to me.

I never wanted my parents to be concerned about me, because Terri's "perfect" and always fine. And for a long time it sure looked that way. I did my best to please people, but in my efforts to please God, I was weak. When temptation came, I fell—more often than I'd like to admit. More than anything, I didn't want to disappoint God, but I didn't know how to be strong against Satan. Although having premarital sex was obviously not the only sin I ever committed, it was the biggest sin that others discovered. For sure, it changed me.

I remember not knowing who I was anymore. I lost my true identity. I didn't know how to act. I used to be perceived as the *good girl*, but overnight I became the *bad girl*. I was confused. I was tormented. I was insecure. I lost the vision for my life. I tried my best to go on with life as usual.

As I sat on my bedroom floor the night I found out I was pregnant, and gasped for breath between my sobs, I painfully wrote the most shocking letter to my parents. I told them their little girl was pregnant outside of marriage. I apologized for being a disgrace and suggested they should disown me. Deep down inside, it was a cry for love.

Oh, how I dreaded my mother checking her mailbox that rainy day, knowing exactly when my letter would arrive! My sweet mom, however, handled the situation with more grace and love than I could imagine. Her first reaction was, "I got your letter today." I said, "You did?" (By now I was sobbing uncontrollably). Then she said, "It looks like we're going to have a grandbaby."

Wow! Only a woman of God would communicate such love and forgiveness at a time when she was so disappointed and hurting. She and my dad both were living examples of the way God loves us even when we disappoint Him. They were quick to forgive me, and I knew that only God could have given them that kind of mercy to handle my news the way they did. I vividly remember my dad calling me, after he received the news from my mom, all the way from a hotel room in Wales.

Through the long distance telephone call, I heard him say, "Terri, this is your daddy." As tears of shame rolled down my face, I cried, "I'm sorry, Daddy. I'm so sorry." I'll never forget his words back to me: "You're going to be all right. Daddy still loves you. You're not the first girl to go through this, and you won't be the last. The Savelles are not quitters, and we're going to get through this."

Hiding many tears, I'm sure, my mom and dad both did their best to show me love and forgiveness. God definitely strengthened my parents to be able to say those words to me at a time when I'm sure they felt broken beyond words. There was no doubt that they loved me. It was clearly spoken. But it didn't change how I felt about myself.

Three weeks later, I walked down a church aisle wearing my sister's wedding dress. Almost the entire time, my head was dropped down in shame. I was paranoid that everyone was staring at my stomach to see proof that I was pregnant (though you couldn't even tell). It was the dream day of every little girl, but I hated every minute of it. I felt like such a failure.

Three weeks later, my baby died.

Wondering what else could possibly go wrong with my "former" perfect life, I lay in a cold hospital room after having surgery to remove my stillborn baby. I looked at the tiny child on the sonogram and wished it had been me that died instead.

What Are You Not Letting Go Of?

Choosing to go on with life and trying to make the best of it, I graduated with honors from college that challenging semester and moved to Fort Worth with my new husband, Rodney. There we started a new life together.

After substitute teaching for a while, I pursued a job at my dad's ministry and began ghostwriting his books. I gained experience in different departments of his ministry and eventually began traveling on crusades with him and another evangelist named Jesse Duplantis.

It appeared that I was over the past. My parents forgave me. I was married. I was justified in the sight of others. I was working in the ministry. I was doing great. Oh the sting of false appearances!

In the summer after I moved to Fort Worth, I attended a Kenneth Copeland Believers' Convention in Anaheim, California. As I stood during the praise and worship service, in the second row, behind my parents, Reverend Oral Roberts was escorted in. He was seated right in front of me and next to my parents.

My dad said to Mr. Roberts, "Do you remember my daughter Terri?"

Mr. Roberts turned around and hugged me. Then he stared at me intently for a long time. Pointing his finger in my face, he said, "Terri, you're called, aren't you?"

I gave him a sheepish smile and responded unconvincingly, "I think so?"

He looked right into my eyes and said, "There's something you're not letting go of! Lift your hands."

I raised both hands and he began hitting the bottom of my elbows and repeating in a booming voice, "Let go! Let go! Let go!"

I stood there crying. I was so embarrased. I knew that people all around me could hear him. I saw the TV cameras homing in on us, and because it was Oral Roberts, people wanted to know what he was saying. I was already full of such shame, I got mad inside. Why couldn't I hear something amazing like, "God has a special plan for your life"? You want to know why? Because God knew what I *really* needed to hear.

I went back to my hotel room that night and went into the bathroom and locked the door. I didn't want my husband to see me. I just wanted to cry. I wanted God to tell me exactly what Mr. Roberts was talking about.

I didn't get my answer that night. The truth was, I was oblivious to what I could be holding on to. It wasn't until I flew back home to Texas, and was out walking one morning, that I found out. Yet again, I begged God to show me what I needed to let go of. All of a sudden, I heard the Lord speak to me inside my spirit. "It's the shame of your past, Terri. It's time to let it go." It wasn't just the shame of getting pregnant that I needed to let go of, it was everything—even those hidden things that nobody knew about. I cried for hours.

I didn't realize that I was carrying so much inside. I was letting my past define me. I was letting it shape my character. I was looking at myself as "the girl who got pregnant" not "the girl who was forgiven." I wasn't as funny as I used to be. I was becoming an introverted, insecure girl.

Only months after that experience with Oral Roberts, I heard Pastor Mac Hammond say that "shame and guilt will keep you from your calling." Now it made sense. You see, Satan doesn't want you doing what you were put on this earth to do. If he can convince you that not only have you sinned, but you *are* that sin, then you will never have the confidence to do anything significant for God. Why? Because sin makes cowards of men: "Fear made cowards of them all" (Esther 9:2, *THE MESSAGE*). If Satan can keep you full of shame, he can keep you from God and His plan for your life.

Satan will do anything he can to stop the plan of God for your life. If it's guilt over the past, he'll use it, just as he did with the man who fell into sexual sin in 2 Corinthians 2:6-7: "The punishment inflicted on him by the majority is sufficient for him. Now instead, you ought to forgive and comfort him, so that he will not be overwhelmed by excessive sorrow" (*NIV*). If it's a past relationship that you know full well God does not want you in, Satan will try to drag you back into it. If you have been delivered from past temptations, Satan will try to convince you to go back to that place.

Is it coincidental? Absolutely not! It's part of the warfare we are in. Nothing about Satan's attacks on your life are by accident. He purposely assaults the areas in your life that hurt you the most. If Satan knows he can intimidate you in an area, he will.

What is it that you need to let go of? What memories are you still replaying over and over in your mind? What are you still holding on to? Picture God standing before you, cupping your face in His gentle hands, and saying, "Let go, My child! Let go! Let go!"

I have fallen into many carefully laid traps that Satan has set before me, and I wish, more than anything, that I hadn't. I wish I had been strong enough to resist temptation before it got me. I wish I had been wise enough to stay focused. I wish I had been confident enough to stand up for myself. I have let myself down more times than I care to remember, and I've had to "let go" of many such painful attachments, many times. But I know what restoration is. I know what healing is. And I know what it takes to keep the past where it belongs . . . in the past.

Conquer Your Past by Focusing on Your Future

I can't tell you how many times I've gotten quiet before the Lord and sat with my journal in my hands ready to write anything I might hear Him say. You know what I would consistently hear in my heart? Yep, that's right. "Let go of the past!"

Weeks would go by. "Let go of the past, Terri!" Months would go by. "Let go of the past, Terri." Years would go by. "Let go of the past, Terri." That was well and good, but I didn't know how. One day, I was led to the verse I mentioned previously, written by the apostle Paul:

> But one thing I do: Forgetting what is behind and straining toward what is ahead, I press on toward the goal to win the prize for which God has called me heavenward in Christ Jesus (Phil. 3:13-14, *NIV*).

> *THE MESSAGE* says it this way: "Friends, don't get me wrong: By no means do I count myself an expert in all of this, but I've got my eye on the goal, where God is beckoning us onward—to Jesus. I'm off and running, and I'm not turning back."

It's obvious when you read Paul's famous verse that he understood that in order to "press toward the mark," or to be in God's perfect will for his life, he had to (1) forget the past, and (2) have a vision. This is what God revealed to me in the vision I told you about at the beginning of this chapter.

I like to envision Philippians 3:13-14 in a picture. I'm watching the acrobatic moves of a trapeze artist. She lets go of one bar, does a magnificent flip in the air and quickly grabs hold of another bar that guides her to the platform. If all she did was let go of the first bar, she'd fall down to the bottom. She has to quickly grab hold of something else to get to the other side.

It's quite an accomplishment to finally let go of your past, but that's not enough. You must quickly grab hold of your future. In other words, you must get a vision for your life if you're ever going to successfully get beyond your past. If you don't have a vision, I can almost guarantee that you will always return to your past, whether it was a life of drugs, alcoholism, homosexuality, crime, infidelity, an unhealthy relationship, or whatever.

The good news is that you can let go of your past and forge ahead with a vision. There is nothing that can stop you. It doesn't matter how old you are. It doesn't matter how educated you are. It doesn't matter what your past experiences have been. It doesn't matter how talented you are. I don't care how small your vision is. If it's to get your laundry done, great! At least you have a vision.

At the end of this book, I have outlined a "chapter challenge" for you to make your dreams bigger than your memories. Every chapter challenge is something I've worked through in my life at some point in time, and I can tell you that it does work. It's important that you put into practice the things you learn, and this is what these chapter challenges help you do. Each challenge helps you stick with the plan of moving toward your future.

Before you panic and think this is just another "write your vision and make it plain" book, I want to give you a very compelling and simple way to come to grips with your true vision. I want to help you write your story and then live it out. First, you need to see what Habakkuk wrote and get those words ingrained in your mind: "And then GOD answered: 'Write this. Write what you see. Write it out in big block letters so that it can be read on the run'" (Hab. 2:2, *THE MESSAGE*).

It's obvious that the Lord knows the power in writing a vision, a dream, a goal. This is why He wrote about it in His Word. Vision stops distraction. Think of it this way: When you write a list of things to buy before you go into a grocery store, it keeps you focused on purchasing just those items. You get in and out a whole lot quicker as you check each item off. If you don't have a list, what tends to happen? That's right. You end up wandering aimlessly down each aisle, grabbing whatever meets your fancy. You waste time and money you don't have, and you'll regret it later. Writing a vision will save you a lot of time, money, energy and emotions.

Having a vision for your life is vital to living your life with purpose versus just existing. God did not create you for the purpose of taking up space. He hand-designed you for a specific purpose. Your job is to discover that purpose, get a plan and pursue it. Many people never take the time to think about their dreams, much less write them down. Those who do are significantly more successful and happier.

Proverbs tells us that without a vision, we will perish (see Prov. 29:18). There's no confusion about that verse. You *will* perish if you do not have a vision for your life. "Perish" means die, decease, pass away, expire, kick the bucket, cash in one's chips, give up the ghost, drop dead, pop off, choke, croak, die out, die off and die down. Okay, some of those sound pretty funny, but we're talking about *your life!* You only have an allotted time on earth. You're going to spend more time on the other side of death than you will here on earth. In the big scope of life, your time on earth really isn't that much! Why would you want to waste your life tormented by a past that you can't do anything about?

You can't change what has happened to you. You can't change what you did. You can't change the choices you made. But the past is over. God wants to use you . . . now! He is incapable of making mistakes. And He made you for a purpose. "For I know the plans I have for you," declares the LORD, "plans to prosper you and not to harm you, plans to give you hope and a future" (Jer. 29:11, *NIV*).

God created you because He needs you. He needs your mouth to speak for Him. He needs your hands to pick others up who are down. He needs your feet to go where others won't go. He needs your trials to be turned into a testimony for someone else to hear. He created you to live out your dreams, not die with them still in you. Determine right now that you are not going to be a person who had a lot of untapped potential, but a person who has potential and chooses to tap into it.

You may be thinking, *I don't know my vision. I've tried to write it, but I don't even know what I'm supposed to do, much less what God's plan is for my life.* I understand. My biggest dreams were to become a Dallas Cowboys cheerleader! I was a big dreamer!

I want to share a story with you that led me to discover how we all can come to grips with our true dreams and goals for life. After you read it, I don't believe you'll ever question again what you really want to accomplish during the time you have left on earth.

Your Funeral

One October morning during my junior year of high school, my English teacher, Mrs. Sawyer, told the class to get out a sheet of paper. She said, "Write your full name at the top. Underneath your name, write your birthdate and last night's date." She paused for a minute, then continued, "Now, I want each of you to write your very own obituary."

What? Isn't that morbid? That's creepy, I thought. I looked around at the other students and we looked at each other, not knowing what to write.

We weren't let off the hook. "C'mon, people," Mrs. Sawyer said. "What do you want people to say about you at your funeral? Give it some thought. Don't write what you've done up to this time in your life. Write what you *want* said about you."

This strange yet sobering assignment came about through a tragic incident that had happened the night before. It was homecoming week, and as tradition would have it, a bunch of the students were "painting the town." The cheerleaders were out that night decorating the houses of each football player. Other students were driving up and down the city streets, cruising the Sonic Drive-In and acting wild. If you're not familiar with homecoming traditions in many schools in the South, the students go all out to show their school spirit.

As cheerleaders, our job was to promote school spirit. And that's exactly what we did. My best friend, Theresa, and I were out in my convertible with the top down. The music was blaring and we were chatting away. In the midst of all the streamers, the paint and high school students looking for an excuse to get out of the house on a school night, tragedy struck. A friendly, likable, Christian guy named Paul accidentally fell out of the back of a truck right in front of the school and was run over. He died later that night.

The next morning, Homecoming Day, the school was silent. It was shocking, unexpected and devastating to us all. I vividly remember walking the halls that day, uniform on, ribbons for sale, the day of the biggest game. The atmosphere felt numb. Nobody was smiling or cheering. Nobody was even "there," for that matter.

So there we were, listening to Mrs. Sawyer's instructions on how to write our own obituary. At the end of class, as she walked around the room to collect the pieces of paper, she told us, "Students, you have just written not your obituary but your dreams. Now live them."

Wow! What a profound project! This exercise is not for high school students alone; it's for anyone and everyone to consider.

Nearly 20 years later, I discovered that Stephen Covey, in his best-selling book *The 7 Habits of Highly Effective People*, listed writing your obituary as one of the habits of successful people! It's the equivalent of writing a vision statement.

When you come to the end of your life and look back, what do you want people to say about you? Would they, right now, say what you want them to say? Or would they not say much at all? How would they describe you? What would they say you did during your time on earth? Did you make a difference in anyone's life?

Forget what they might say right now; what do you *want* them to say? What do you want to accomplish if age, money, education and past experiences were no factor? Don't analyze it, and for goodness' sake, don't try to figure out how it could possibly happen to you. That's not the point. The point is to dream. Later on in this book, I will help you develop a daily vision for your life that will lead you right into God's perfect plan; but for now, I want you to get your mind off of the past and onto your future by dreaming big, with no limits, no excuses, no boundaries.

Just dream.

I'm giving you permission to dream as big as you possibly can. And don't fear that others might read it and make fun of you. Who cares? It's your life, and you only live it once. Imagine that your life is over and the person closest to you has been asked to write your obituary. What would you want them to write? Go ahead and write it for them.

Don't rush through this for the purpose of moving on to chapter 2. Take your time, sit down, think it through and write.

I have done this myself and found that it helped tremendously in following a vision for my life. I took the time to just be honest with myself and write. I didn't write with the thought that anyone else might read it and it would embarrass me. I just wrote how I would like to be described and what I would like to have accomplished. I didn't finish it in one day or even two. I wrote it in increments, but my goal was to finish it, and I did. I wrote my dreams.

Now it's time for you to write yours.

2

WHEN PAIN BRINGS YOU TO YOUR KNEES ... *YOU CAN BE HEALED THERE*

I remember well the period of my life when the vision I had was lost. I was a youth pastor who had big dreams for the most dynamic youth ministry in Texas! I dreamed of busing teenagers in from all over the Dallas/Fort Worth Metroplex. I could imagine a giant warehouse with rock-climbing walls, skateboard parks, basketball courts all filled with passionate young people whose lives we could powerfully influence. And I was heading toward that dream. My husband and I even purchased the giant warehouse and began making preliminary plans. In the process, however, my marriage was completely falling apart. *I* was falling apart.

It may seem as if my marriage was in jeopardy overnight, but the reality was a gradual decline over a period of years. Nobody knew the pain, dysfunction and unresolved issues my husband and I kept under wraps. We were both working two jobs, and our stress rose to alarming levels. Unable to make any headway in our relationship, we separated. We resigned as youth pastors and also resigned our vision.

I was asked to work from home for a period of time, which I thought was the worst thing in the world for me. I love being around people and always hated being alone. On the first morning, I took my daughter to school and returned to my empty house. I didn't know what to do. I felt so empty and useless. Every dream I had for our youth ministry was gone. All those Wednesday nights of ministering and preparing messages were over. All the summer camp planning and girl sleepovers at my house were over. I felt my dreams were over.

As you discovered in reading the first chapter that a person with no vision will always return to his or her past, you can be assured that my past was directly in front of me. The desire and temptation to leave everything was so strong and nearly overpowering that it was an intense fight for my life to get to where I'm at today.

I remember driving home one dark and rainy night, wrestling with my emotions. I couldn't go home just yet. I was hurting too bad to compose myself and fake it until I pulled it together. So I pulled into a cul-de-sac in the front of my neighborhood and parked there. I left the car running and leaned my head against the steering wheel and just cried from the deepest part of my guts.

I felt so alone.

The Battle You Can't See

There are some things that have to be settled in your heart right from the beginning so that you'll have a better understanding of the tough things you go through in life. We all know that bad things happen even to good people. It doesn't matter if you are a Christian or not; sometimes life is hard. But as believers, we need to be aware that we have a good God in the midst of even the most horrible circumstances. We need to learn how to overcome those circumstances with Him.

You are in a war. It's not a war that you can see with your natural eyes. It's not a war that you can fight with your hands. It's a spiritual war. Paul said in Ephesians 6:12 that "For our struggle is not against flesh and blood, but against the rulers, against the authorities, against the powers of this dark world and against the spiritual forces of evil in the heavenly realms" (*NIV*). God is on your side to help you win this war. He's given you every spiritual weapon you will ever need to outlast the enemy, but you have to pick them up and use them. (I'll talk about this later on in the book.)

The war on the enemy's side is headed by Satan. He is not a Halloween character or a figure dressed in a red costume with a pitchfork. He's a real enemy who has one plan for your life: to kill, steal and destroy you! John warned us, "The thief comes only in order to steal and kill and destroy. I [Jesus] came that they may have and enjoy life, and have it in abundance (to the full, till it overflows)" (John 10:10, *AMP*).

My dad explains that verse this way: "You have to understand that there is a spiritual line drawn in your life. On one side is God, who gives you everything good. On the other side is the devil, who brings the bad stuff. Don't ever cross the two. You must have a firm conviction about this so you can trust your loving, heavenly Father who has designed a good plan for your life."

The devastating things you've been through are not coincidental. Satan is a master deceiver, and he has a well-thought-out plot to destroy *every* child of God. Reader, he hates you! He hates what you stand for. He hates the God you serve. He would love nothing more than to stop your future. And he knows exactly how to do this—by keeping you trapped in your past. He will either torment you about it or drag you back into it by using the tools of guilt, shame, condemnation, self-pity, loneliness or bitterness.

Your past has a way of shaping who you are today. It's amazing how one single dramatic experience of rejection in childhood can last throughout adulthood and forever alter your self-image. It's not until you truly get a revelation of who you are in Christ and apply it to your life that your past can be erased and a new image of yourself be formed.

I was talking to a woman who worked at a tanning salon, and I mentioned to her that I had just returned from my first missions trip to Costa Rica. She asked what I spoke about, and I said, "What to do when you're hurting." I went on to tell her that so many of us, including myself, have suffered with low self-esteem. Before I could finish the sentence she remarked, "Low self-esteem? Try *no* self-esteem."

This woman spent the next several minutes telling me about her horrific past. My heart broke over every word she spoke. She was sexually abused by her father, her uncle and her neighbor. It seemed that no matter where she went in life, she found herself in abusive relationships. Her past has shaped who she is today. She sees herself through the eyes of a person that has no value in life.

This is how Satan can destroy you. He has an overall plan to keep you so locked into what happened to you way back then that you will never have the confidence to step out and do what God wants you to do today.

You Are Not Alone

During the time my marriage was falling apart, I dreaded going home to an empty house. I didn't realize the root behind my fear of being alone. See, the more you're around people, the less time you have to just be quiet and think. I didn't want to think of how messed up my heart and my thoughts had become. It was too painful. As long as I kept busy and surrounded myself with people, I could hide the pain for a while. As long as I was involved in a web of activity, I could still function without needing to be honest with myself about my future.

But when the church services were over, when the friends left, when the office was closed, there was no way to hide my loneliness. I had to face the reality of my situation. You may understand what I'm talking about. Perhaps you have a rich social life or a great marriage or a great job, but you still feel alone. Let me encourage you that no matter how bad it gets, you are never alone. This time in your life can be a gift that God can use to remove all the distractions and draw you closer to Him.

When David was alone with God on the backside of the wilderness with his flocks—his alone time with God—his heart became strong in the Lord, and he became a giant-slayer (see 1 Sam. 17:32-36). I have discovered that my healing, my restoration and the wholeness I now have in my heart are a direct result of being alone. It was in my alone time that I was forced to be honest with myself about the decisions I was making. It was in my alone time that I came to grips with what I was going to do with the rest of my life. It was in my alone time that I cried out to God, genuinely received His love and was made whole from the inside out. You may be suffering with thoughts of feeling alone, but I want you to know that it's the best place to be.

During that time of aloneness, I was reminded of the need to write a vision, but the thought was overwhelming. I couldn't even think about writing a big vision for my life; I needed a small vision for the next hour! I sat down at my desk and began working on a vision for when I woke up the next morning. It was simple: I was to set aside some alone time to be with God. I had to fight this battle by spending alone time in prayer, worship and praise.

Second Chronicles 20:15 tells us, "The Lord says this to you: Be not afraid or dismayed at this great multitude; for the battle is not yours, but God's" (*AMP*). I knew I had to fight this battle by trusting God to heal my life. I knew I needed to pray. I knew I needed that release in my life. I knew I needed to just get on my knees and worship God without a soundtrack of distractions. Still, I dreaded silence. As long as I could hear a preacher preaching in the background, I didn't feel alone. But to just sit quietly in a room and cry out to God? It seemed very lonely. But I didn't give up.

The first morning that I decided to spend alone time with God, I took my daughter to school, drove home, walked into my house, laid my keys on the kitchen counter and looked around, thinking, *Now what do I do?* God wasn't physically standing in my kitchen with me. I couldn't see Him. I couldn't hear Him. I could not even feel Him.

I didn't realize at the time how dependent I was on other people to be what only God could be in my life. I wanted *a person* to never leave me nor forsake me. I wanted *a person* to hold me. I wanted *a person* to comfort me, help me, lead me and build me up. But it was only the Holy Spirit, of course, who could do those things.

Perhaps you are like I was. Maybe you have a dependent personality and have the tendency to lean on people to take care of you, instead of leaning on God. Maybe you trust in people instead of God. Maybe you ask for people to guide you instead of God. *Stop!* Embrace God. Let Him be what only He can be in your life. Stop looking to others for something they are incapable of being to you.

I know it isn't easy to allow God to comfort you when you can't physically feel Him. Sometimes you just want that feeling of being held. It makes you feel safe. It gives you that sense that everything is okay. In my life, I had to fight this loneliness with a plan. I had to get things right inside or they would never be right outside. I began learning that my "battle position" in this spiritual war was actually in worshiping God.

In other words, God would fight the battle for me as long as I kept my eyes on Him by worshiping Him. "For we have no might to stand against this great company that is coming against us. We do not know what to do, but our eyes are upon You" (2 Chron. 20:12, *AMP*).

The Power of the Presence of God

I started out doing all of this out of desperation rather than pure devotion and love for God. But who could blame me? I was hurting, and I was in desperate need of a Healer.

Then something incredible happened. The more I read my Bible, the more I learned. The more I learned, the more I applied His

Word to my life. The more I applied His Word to my life, the more I came to God with a pure spirit. Every morning I was committed to spending time with Him in my den, praying and worshiping Him with a CD of music playing in the background. I was creating an environment that not only brought peace to my soul but also welcomed the presence of God.

I began worshiping Him for the very things I needed the most: peace, strength, comfort, wisdom and healing. I would magnify *Him* rather than magnify my messed-up life. I worshiped Him for His very attributes that I needed the most in my life: Jehovah-Rapha (our Healer), the Deliverer, the Prince of Peace, the Strong Tower, the Hiding Place, the Redeemer and the Restorer of my soul.

Sometimes reciting the same prayers for help gets old after a while. God hears us the first time we ask. So sometimes it's best to just focus on Him and how awesome He is, instead of asking Him for something He already knows about. There is a lot of power in praise. As I bowed down day after day and gave myself to Him in praise and worship, something began to change. *Me!* I gradually experienced the true healing power of Jesus *on my knees.* I am proof that when the pain brings you to your knees, you can be healed there.

Nothing changed overnight; it wasn't an immediate transformation. But eventually my morning worship time became the place where my heart, day after day, began to be molded and take the shape of a fully healed heart.

I wasn't doing it out of obligation anymore. I truly looked forward to spending alone time with God. I felt safe in His presence.

God wants you to feel that too. He wants you to worship Him, to voice your love for Him and to sincerely trust Him right now. He wants to bring healing to your life.

Scripture says of God, "Thou that inhabitest the praises of Israel" (Ps. 22:3, *KJV*). "Inhabit" means to live, dwell and abide in. When you offer God praise and worship, He's right there. You are speaking His language! When you open your mouth and say, "Lord, I love You. I worship You. You're powerful. You're strong. You're faithful. I trust You, Lord. I need You right now. I depend on You. You never leave me nor forsake me, and I thank you, Father, for being my Healer," you automatically get God's full attention.

What happens in God's presence? The Bible tells us that strength and joy are found there (see 1 Chron. 16:27). That's exactly what you need as you get a new vision for your life. You need joy rising up in you. You need strength moving you forward. Nehemiah 8:10 tells us, "The joy of the LORD is your strength" (*NKJV*). Strength for what? To overcome what has been overcoming you; to battle against temptation, distractions, depression, torment, anxiety and confusion.

You may be in a situation right now where things have changed and your vision has either shifted or is completely gone. You may feel that your life has come to that fork in the road where you are about to make some big decisions. Either you're going all the way with God's plan for your life or you're going with what you *feel*. I'm telling you right now that you will always regret living by what you feel. *Always*. Your feelings will lie to you. Your feelings will lead you out of God's perfect plan for your life. Your feelings will deceive you into thinking it's what you really want.

You may be going through something in your life that you haven't told a soul and you know it's a battle that's sabotaging your spiritual life. You may be holding on to a lot of fear, and nobody knows exactly what you've been through. I want you to know that God knows. He sees your pain. He understands. And He wants you to focus on Him so that He can bring you out of your pain.

Remember, God cannot use you publicly until you have gotten victory privately. You must be established in your place with God alone. Nobody around. Nobody watching. Just you and Him. You need His presence to deliver you, heal you and restore everything that has been stolen in your life. God *will* restore the years that Satan stole from you (see Joel 2:25). He will restore your joy. He will restore your vision. He will restore your marriage. He will restore your hope. He will restore your finances. He will restore your self-esteem. He will do all things, because there is power in His presence.

To receive these things, you must accept the love and forgiveness God has for you. There is nothing you can do to earn it. Nothing. You can't go to church so many times that finally your sins are erased. You can't pray for so many hours that the past is finally removed. There is no formula or method to apply other than choosing to *receive* it or *reject* it. If you want to let go of your past, you must learn to take in the love He is offering.

51

It doesn't matter what you have done in your life or how big you think your sins are in comparison to someone else's sins. Proverbs 10:12 tells us that "love covers all sins" (*NKJV*). Yes, even yours!

No Need to Hide

After Adam and Eve sinned in the Garden and hid from God because they were afraid, God didn't change. Adam and Eve changed, but God's character remained the same. He was still the same God who loved them and wanted to commune with them. He was the same God who gave them good gifts. He was the same God who wanted them to succeed. But because they were covered in shame, they turned away from Him.

We do the same thing today. We sin or give in to a temptation over and over, and what happens? We feel ashamed. We feel heavy inside. We avoid God. And we are unable to ignore the emptiness we still feel in our hearts. I am so encouraged by this verse in Romans: "For God's gifts and His call are irrevocable. [He never withdraws them when once they are given, and He does not change His mind about those to whom He gives His grace or to whom He sends His call]" (Rom. 11:29, *AMP*).

God doesn't change. We are the ones that change. God was, is and will always be love. His love is unconditional. It is not based on your meeting all the conditions of being perfect. He knows that not one of us can be perfect, but He still loves us.

What are you ashamed of that is causing you to hide from God? What experiences are you too ashamed to talk to the Lord about? Jesus said, "For everyone practicing evil hates the light and does not come to the light, lest his deeds should be exposed. But he who does the truth comes to the light, that his deeds may be clearly seen, that they have been done in God" (John 3:20-21, *NKJV*). You know, as long as you're hiding something, Satan has power over you. You're being defeated when you simply don't have to be.

You can't hide from God, because He sees everything. He is omniscient, which means He is everywhere at once. He has witnessed every experience you have ever been through. He has heard your desperate cries. He sees your scars. He sees your struggle with low self-esteem.

You and your experiences are not a surprise to Him. What He wants is for you to stop hiding and come into the light of His presence so that He can pour His love into your life. His love is what can change every single area of your life.

God's unfailing love is a mystery to me. I often wonder why He is so loving and forgiving when we are so selfish. You know why? Because He can't help it. It's His nature. In Exodus 34:6-7, the Lord tells Moses that the essence of His name and nature is compassion and holiness: "The LORD passed before him and proclaimed, 'The LORD, the LORD God, merciful and gracious, longsuffering, and abounding in goodness and truth, keeping mercy for thousands, forgiving iniquity and transgression and sin, by no means clearing *the guilty,* visiting the iniquity of the fathers upon the children'" (*NKJV*). And in Psalm 36:5-6, David says, "God's love is meteoric, His loyalty astronomic, His purpose titanic, His verdict oceanic. Yet in his largeness nothing gets lost; not a man, not a mouse, slips through the cracks" (*THE MESSAGE*). God doesn't try to be loving. He simply *is* love.

When you understand the God who loves you unconditionally, you are better motivated to spend time with Him out of pure devotion. I don't believe you can genuinely communicate under the guise of force. If you are being told, "You better pray. You better worship. You better praise," I'm sure it's the last thing you are going to want to do. But when you understand that God adores you and longs for you, and you receive that gift, you are going to want to be with Him.

Take this moment to absorb the truth of the absolute love of Jesus directed toward you, as communicated in Romans 8:35,37-39, *THE MESSAGE*:

Do you think anyone is going to be able to drive a wedge between us and Christ's love for us? There is no way! Not trouble, not hard times, not hatred, not hunger, not homelessness, not bullying threats, not backstabbing, not even the worst sins listed in Scripture. . . . None of this fazes us because Jesus loves us. I'm absolutely convinced that nothing—nothing living or dead, angelic or demonic, today or tomorrow, high or low, thinkable or unthinkable—absolutely nothing can get between us and God's love because of the way that Jesus our Master has *embraced* us.

Accept that God loves you, and make His Word the final authority in your life. Don't listen to the lies of Satan. Worship God consistently, even when you don't feel like it, and always thank Him for loving you.

Listen for Him

In John 10:27, Jesus promised that we would hear His voice: "My sheep listen to My voice; I know them, and they follow Me." Jesus also said that the Holy Spirit would teach us (see John 14:26) and would speak to us (see John 16:12). The Early Church regularly listened to the Holy Spirit's direction and counsel (see Acts 15:28). David waited for the Lord to speak to his heart and gained strength from listening to the Lord: "I will praise the LORD, who counsels me; even at night my heart instructs me. I have set the LORD always before me. Because He is at my right hand, I will not be shaken" (Ps. 16:7-8, *NIV*).

A lot of my alone time was spent getting quiet and listening to God. I wanted to hear His voice so badly, but I doubted that He would even want to talk to me. After all, I had made so many mistakes. *Why would Almighty God want to talk to me?* I wondered. But I kept waiting for His voice. And I kept hearing nothing.

One day, as I was just kneeling, listening intently, I heard in my heart, *I love you, Terri.* I thought, *Who was that? That had to be me!* But then again, I wasn't real pleased with myself at that time. I wouldn't say that I loved myself. I thought about it further. *I know the devil doesn't love me. His plan is to kill, steal and destroy my life.* I realized it *had* to be God! I broke. I could not hold back the uncontrollable tears of so much pain and so much junk that I had kept inside for too many years. I began pouring it all out. Everything.

In the midst of my sobs, I would hear, "Terri, I love you." The more I heard those words, the more I wanted to worship Him and praise Him. It was such an incredible experience. There I was, sitting in the den of my house, with no one around, and the God who created this universe was saying He loves me! Those words changed my entire destiny! I still couldn't understand why He would love me at that time in my life. I knew I didn't deserve His love, but He kept telling me He did. Who was I to say otherwise?

I was reminded of the verse "The righteous cry out, and the LORD hears them; he delivers them from all their troubles. The LORD is close to the brokenhearted, and saves those who are crushed in spirit" (Ps. 34:17-18, *NIV*).

If that passage of Scripture describes you, all you have to do is cry out to God and He is right there with His love. No matter what. No matter when.

Are you crushed in spirit?

Are you brokenhearted?

Are you feeling abandoned or rejected?

Are you lonely?

Are you tormented?

Do you feel like giving up?

Do you think nobody cares about you?

It's okay. God loves you and is just waiting for you to call on Him.

When you do, you must listen for His voice deep in your heart. He wants to speak to you even more than you want to listen. He doesn't want you spending your life guessing what His plans are for you. He wants to tell you. He just needs you to listen. He needs your confidence built up to such a place that you know that you know the voice of God. And how does that happen? By spending time with Him.

The more time you spend with someone, the more you know that person's voice. My husband can call me at work and I don't have to ask who is on the line. Because I have spent so much time with him, I know his voice. I'm not confused at all, even when he prank calls me! (I know his disguised voices, too.) The more time you spend with someone, the more you will recognize his voice. If you set aside time for God, if you invite His presence into your life, if you set the stage for Him to speak to you, He will!

To capture those times when God is speaking to you, I highly recommend getting a journal to write in. I call mine a "Quiet Time" journal, and I use one based on this verse: "Write all the words that I have spoken to you in a book" (Jer. 30:2, *AMP*). Spending some time in worship and praise seems to prepare you more for hearing His voice. It's not a method or a mandatory routine by any means, but for me worship and praise help get all the junk off my mind and open my heart up to hear His voice.

Then sit quietly in His presence and just listen. God gave you two ears and one mouth for a reason. He wants you to listen twice as much as you talk. Don't always feel that you need to talk during your quiet time with God. Just listen. Yes, you will most likely hear your own thoughts rolling around in your head and wonder, *Is that God? Or is it just me?* Whatever you hear, write it down. Don't get discouraged if you don't get anything right away or the first few times you listen. It might take a few tries to learn to dial down and quiet your heart and mind enough to be sensitive to the Holy Spirit. Job 33:14 states, "For God does speak—now one way, now another—though man may not perceive it" (*NKJV*).

At first you may feel uncertain whether a thought, word, picture or impression is from you or from God. If so, you're in good company. Even Jeremiah the prophet was uncertain in one case of what God was saying to him (see Jer. 32:6-7). It wasn't until after Jeremiah received external confirmation in his circumstances that he could say, "Then I knew that this was the word of the LORD" (Jer. 32:8, *NKJV*). Up until this time, Jeremiah *did not know for sure* if what he had heard was from God. So if you feel uncertain about what you hear as you wait on the Lord, trust that what you heard came from Him and then examine whatever you have received against Scripture to discern anything that may not be from God. Remember that God will never say something that contradicts His Word (see Isa. 8:20).

In 1 Thessalonians 5:20-21, Paul says, "Do not treat prophecies with contempt. Test everything. Hold on to the good" (*NIV*). You can use the following questions to test whether what you have heard is from the Lord:

1. Does it bring glory to Jesus (see 1 Cor. 12:3; John 16:14)?
2. Would Jesus do or say what you have heard (see 1 Cor. 11:1)?
3. Is it in harmony with Scripture (see Isa. 8:20)?
4. Does it build you up in faith (see 1 Cor. 14:3-5)?

I write down whatever comes up in my spirit, whether I think it's me or I think it's God. There have been many times when I wrote whatever I felt in my spirit, and the whole time I was saying to myself, *That is you, Terri! It's not God!* Then I would read the journal a few days later and think, *Oh my goodness. That had to be God. I would never come up with something that good.*

Open Your Mouth and Sing!

Did you know that praising God is a form of spiritual warfare? Psalm 149:6 says, "May the praise of God be in their mouths and a double-edged sword in their hands" (*NIV*). You may not feel like singing, or you may not have perfect pitch; but it doesn't matter. You will do damage to Satan's kingdom when you open your mouth and sing. Psalm 22:3 says that the Lord's very presence and power come and inhabit our praises. When God shows up in power, Satan and his demons have no choice but to flee. As James states, "Submit yourselves, then, to God. Resist the devil, and he will flee from you. Come near to God, and He will come near to you" (Jas. 4:7-8, *NIV*).

Singing to the Lord brings up a very powerful memory in my mind. It proved to be a turning point (spiritually speaking) in my hardest hours, which I didn't even realize at the time. It happened on a Friday afternoon, on the first weekend that my daughter was going to spend away from me at her father's temporary residence. I was so used to picking her up from school and spending my entire weekend with her, and now she was spending weekends with her father.

Everything had changed in my life. I had developed a plan during the weekdays to keep me busy and focused on my goals and hearing the Word; but to think of spending Friday and Saturday night alone—without my daughter—filled me with dread.

After I dropped her off at her dad's place, I sat at the bottom of the steps of my house with my head in my hands. I hated my life. I hated everything about it. And I didn't see a way out.

As I sat there feeling sorry for myself, confused and sinking more and more into depression, I realized it wasn't a total lost cause. Satan couldn't totally have his way with me. All of those mornings of hearing the Word and worshiping God weren't in vain! A glimmer of hope flickered inside of me and the Word began to rise up in me. Sure, God was doing a work, but I also had to cooperate with Him. I couldn't continue to wallow in self-pity, keeping the door open for Satan to keep moving in my life.

I wiped my tears and *made* myself lift my hands to heaven. In a shaky voice I began to sing, "Lord, I give You my heart, I give You my soul. I live for You alone. Every breath that I take, every moment I'm awake, Lord, have Your way in me."

That sacrifice of praise slapped the devil in the face! It became the theme song in my life. I continued this act of battle nearly every single day. I did the same thing: I raised my hands and sang to God. The words I sang were what I believed for in my life. I began making up verses to the song with the same tune. I would sing, "Lord, I give You my will. Conform it to Your will. Lead me every single day. I need You more each day. I love You, love You, Father." Over and over and over I would sing to the Lord.

Satan hates to hear your praises to God. It enrages him. That alone should make you want to sing that much more. If your songs will do damage to Satan's kingdom, it should be a clear sign that you should do it. Just open your mouth and sing. Sing out of your spirit. Make up songs to the Lord as you're doing your housework or making dinner. You are not only glorifying God, but you are also putting yourself in a position for God to move on your behalf. You are literally opening the door for Him to change your circumstances, your heart and your life.

There will be some days when you just won't feel like it, but you cannot be ruled by your feelings. You have to get to a place in your life where you absolutely tell your feelings to SHUT UP! Do not let them have any influence over you anymore.

Read one example of what Scripture says happened to the enemies of God's children: "And when they began to sing and to praise, the LORD set ambushments against the men of Ammon, Moab, and Mount Seir who had come against Judah, and they were [self-] slaughtered" (2 Chron. 20:22, *AMP*).

Singing praises to God confuses your enemy! Singing God's praises welcomes His presence and, ultimately, changes you. Make note of some of the worship songs you like to sing when you're at church. Write down the words and take them with you to your quiet time with God. Get it out and begin singing. It's spiritual warfare that will change your life!

Never Underestimate the Power of the Name of Jesus

The entire Bible can be summed up in one word: Jesus. The name of Jesus is *the* most powerful name there is. His name heals the sick: "It is by the name of Jesus Christ of Nazareth, whom you crucified but whom God raised from the dead, that this man stands before you healed" (Acts 4:10). At the mention of His name, demons tremble, nations shake, diseases are cured, hearts are healed, blind eyes are opened and the deaf can hear. There is no other name like the name of Jesus.

Just say the name of Jesus quietly as you sit here reading this book. Say it: "Jesus." There is something about that name. It's indescribable. There's healing in His name. There's wholeness in His name. There's hope in His name. There's joy in His name. There's deliverance in His name. There's peace in His name.

I remember when I was a little girl hearing a story about a lady who was being attacked and nearly raped. She began screaming the name of Jesus, and the attacker fled! We aren't always delivered from every painful circumstance, but we can know with assurance that Jesus is always with us, loving us and comforting us. After hearing that story, I knew that whenever I was in need, as long as I called on the name of Jesus, there was hope. You are never without hope or help when you say that beautiful name.

I saw firsthand how powerful His name is when I ministered on my first missions trip to Costa Rica. The altar call was filled with ladies suffering from sexual abuse, emotional pain and much scarring from their past. I couldn't speak their language, and they couldn't speak mine. I had been using an interpreter while I preached; but when I began to pray over each one of them at the altar, I was on my own. I prayed in English, and they had no idea what I was saying. But as soon as I would say, "In the name of Jesus," something would be released in their spirit. I saw this happen with each woman.

You must realize the power that is in the name of Jesus. In Philippians 2:10, Paul tells us, "At the name of Jesus every knee will bow, of those who are in heaven and on earth and under the earth" (*NASB*). Everything and everyone will eventually submit to His name. In my alone time, I began taking authority over all the things that were tormenting me, by speaking the name of Jesus over them. How? I began declaring these things:

- Depression is a name, and it must bow to the name of Jesus!
- Torment is a name, and it must bow to the name of Jesus!
- Loneliness is a name, and it must bow to the name of Jesus!
- Deception is a name, and it must bow to the name of Jesus!
- Confusion is a name, and it must bow to the name of Jesus!
- Fear is a name, and it must bow to the name of Jesus!

You can do the same thing. In Luke 10:17, the disciples told Jesus, "Lord, even the demons submit to us in Your name" (Luke 10:17, *NIV*). Wherever Satan has a hold in your life—whether it's alcohol, lust, pornography, smoking, lying, controlling spirits, laziness—they must bow to the name of Jesus. It works, but it won't take just one time. You need to keep speaking it out of your mouth every day and make your declarations frequent. Even Jesus Himself had to command some demons repeatedly: "[Jesus] *had been saying to him,* 'Come out of the man, you unclean spirit!'" (Mark 5:8, *NASB*, emphasis added).[1] If Jesus had to repeatedly command Satan, then we will have to do so all the more. I like what Joyce Meyer says: "At least give God as much time as you gave the devil." Consistently, use the name of Jesus at every opportunity. It is your greatest weapon!

Experience God in Your Own Personal Way

Once you develop an intimate relationship with God, you will never be the same. If you have battled with insecurity and inferiority like I have, you will develop confidence you never knew existed. You will be free from timidity, fear, low self-esteem, passivity and feelings of rejection. You will be free from all of the debilitating mindsets that are keeping you from fulfilling your assignment on earth! God will become your best friend, your confidant, the One to whom you talk about everything.

Experiencing God in your own personal way doesn't happen overnight. You don't get to know God by one life-changing encounter. It happens through relationship. We all know that relationships are built over time. The same applies to God. You have to invest yourself, your time and your priorities to being with Him.

James 4:8 tells us, "Come close to God and He will come close to you" (*AMP*). Look who makes the first move—*you*. God waits on *you*. He is the perfect gentleman. God doesn't force Himself on anyone.

God just wants private time with you. "But when you pray, go into your [most] private room, and, closing the door, pray to your Father, Who is in secret; and your Father, Who sees in secret, will reward you in the open" (Matt. 6:6, *AMP*). Go somewhere quiet where no one can bother you, and give your Father your full attention. You'll never be the same again.

If the pain you feel inside literally brings you to your knees, it is the best place to be. On your knees is where you will find a loving, healing Father who wants nothing more than to see your life put together, restored and in line with His perfect plan for you. You can receive that healing by repeating this declaration, "Thank You, Father, for loving me."

Say those words out loud several times a day when you're alone. Get used to hearing it out of your own mouth. What you repeatedly hear, you will eventually believe; and Scripture teaches that as you believe it in your heart, you will actually experience the reality in your life: "As he thinks in his heart, so is he" (see Prov. 23:7, *NKJV*). Every time you declare with your mouth that God loves you, layers of bondage are being stripped away from your life. Shame from the past is being uprooted. Guilt is being washed away.

When you receive God's amazing love for you, you begin to fall in love with Him. And when you fall in love with God, you want to do everything you can to please Him and live a life in accordance with His Word.

God's love can change everything in your life. It can give you the self-worth you have lacked. It can restore your broken dreams. It can instill confidence in your ability to be yourself. It can destroy hurts and wounds that have kept you bound. It can release you from fears that have held you captive all of your life. It is the most foundational principle in the Word of God and is the only channel through which you can be healed.

Accept God's love for you.

Listen for Him.

Open your mouth and sing.

Never underestimate the power of the name of Jesus.

Experience God in your own personal way.

Note

1. The Greek verb translated in the *NASB* as "he had been saying" is *elegen*. See A. T. Robertson, *Studies in Mark's Gospel* (Nashville, TN: Broadman Press, 1958), commentary on Mark 5:8. Max Zerwick, another well-known Greek scholar, also translates the imperfect verb *elegen* with a past continuous meaning: "[for] he had been saying." See *A Grammatical Analysis of the Greek New Testament,* third edition (Rome: Pontifical Biblical Institute, 1988), p. 116; and *Biblical Greek* (Rome: Pontifical Biblical Institute, 1963), p. 290.

3

WHEN YOU ADMIT IT'S BEHIND YOU... *YOU'RE FREE TO MOVE FORWARD*

There's not a day in my life that I feel forgiven for my past. Just this past weekend, I woke up feeling ashamed of things I have done. I even felt like putting a stop to writing this book, being in ministry and especially being an example for others to follow. You might be thinking, *Then why am I trying to learn from you?* Here's why.

You can't live by what your *feelings* tell you. You have to choose to live by what the Word of God says. You will never *feel* forgiven. You just have to *receive* the gift of forgiveness. Easier said than done, right?

How many times have you asked God to forgive you for the *same* sin? How many times of repenting do you think it takes for God to finally say, "Okay, you're forgiven"? Is it 25 times of confession . . . 250 times? What is the magic number of times you must confess your sins to finally *feel* forgiven? How many years does it take to finally receive God's forgiveness? How many sermons do you have to hear before you finally believe that it applies to your life too? I cannot even begin to count how many times I have gone before the Lord and said, "Lord, I ask You to forgive me for *that* again." He must be so tired of hearing it!

In these moments you must remember that you cannot earn what Jesus did for you. You cannot earn what the blood of Jesus bought and paid for in your life, no matter how hard you work. Do you deserve it? Absolutely not. Nobody does. Did you read that? *Nobody.* "There is no one righteous, not even one" (Rom. 3:10, *NIV*). I do not believe that you can go forward toward your future until you choose to apply the following three steps to putting the past behind you:

1. Repent
2. Forgive yourself
3. Forgive others

Forgiveness is such a vital part of letting go of your past. Receiving forgiveness from God and releasing forgiveness toward yourself and others is what will keep you looking ahead instead of behind.

I read a story about an old tribe in Asia who used to yell what they considered the worst curse at their enemy. It was: "May you stay in one place forever!" That's what Satan wants you to do—be still and not move forward. But that is not God's plan for your life. He wants you to progress.

Step 1: Repent

It doesn't matter how good you look on the outside; if you are full of junk on the inside, you will not walk out God's plan for your life. Most of all, you will stay miserable! Most of us have a tendency to look at people "on the outside" and make many false assumptions about them. I think we would be very surprised by what lies on the inside. We would probably see a pile of junk! Stuff that needs to be thrown out. It can be any type of sin that is causing you to stay stagnant in your life and is keeping you from God. It can even be a situation that you were not responsible for but it weighs heavy on your heart.

You may be trying everything you know to do to make the outside look great, but you're still miserable inside. Nothing will change in your life until you get healed on the inside.

It's time to get rid of the heaviness in your heart. It's time to let it all out and receive God's forgiveness for everything you've been carrying around. You cannot fulfill your purpose on earth until you repent and bring everything to the light before God. When you repent, it's the first step toward admitting that your past is finally behind you and you're free to move forward.

> Man looks on the outward appearance, but the Lord looks on the heart (1 Sam. 16:7, *ESV*).

I had a very real experience with trying to cover up a mess on the outside that taught me a powerful lesson. I love to walk. I walk nearly five miles every day. It is a very calming activity for me. One day, I noticed one of my toes on my left foot was very sore. I could not remember hurting it and figured it probably wasn't serious. I assumed it would heal itself quickly. As days went by, the toe got puffy and quite tender.

My then seven-year-old daughter, Kassidi, jumped into my arms one afternoon and, weighing almost as much as me, I dropped her. She landed right on my injured toe. I screamed, and hopped around on one foot in such pain. Evidently, it ruptured, and blood gushed out. Kassidi felt horrible. I assured her that it wasn't her fault, and I told her I had already hurt my toe long before she landed on it. It was the pressure that made the sore burst open.

I bandaged the toe and figured the worst part was over and it would soon heal. I was wrong. Weeks went by, and my toenail turned black and got real thick. It looked disgusting and repulsive. I put some peroxide on it to clean up any infection.

More weeks went by. My toe kept getting worse. Suddenly, another toe on the other foot was beginning to turn the same way. I was confused. What was going on? Did I have an infection on both feet?

After concluding that my infection came from the nail salon where I had just gotten a pedicure, I ran to the drugstore to buy an antibiotic cream. The instructions on the antifungal cream I bought advised applying the cream no more than once or twice daily. I put it on 10 times in 10 minutes! I wanted instant healing! I continued this routine for several weeks, but nothing changed. Finally, a third toe became infected! Not to mention it was SANDAL SEASON!

Finally, I got the bright idea to get my feet checked out by a doctor. He diagnosed a major infection and said it came from walking so much and my toes hitting the end of my running shoes. Then he told me, "This kind of infection must be treated from the inside and will eventually work its way to the outside." No amount of peroxide, creams, soaking or polishing would treat this infection. He repeated, "Terri, it's going to take time!"

"How long?" I asked.

"Possibly six months," he said. "Don't call me in two weeks because your toenail is still black and it looks like nothing is working. It will take a long while to heal." Then he added that I must visit the clinic once a month for the next six months to do blood work to monitor how this medication was affecting my liver and kidneys.

I had to get a prescription filled, take medication, doctor my toes, cover them with Band-Aids and take time out of my busy schedule to make monthly doctor visits so they could poke me with a needle, draw blood and monitor my liver and kidney function! All over a . . . TOE! What appeared to be an insignificant little sore turned out to become a big issue in my life! And, I might add, very costly!

Before I knew how serious this was, I kept polishing my toenails, trying to make them *look* pretty on the outside while a fungus was growing deeper and thicker underneath. Any onlooker, from a distance, would have seen beautiful feet until they got close to me. Polish, bandages, peroxide, and even toe rings couldn't cover what was happening on the inside. The problem had to be dealt with from the inside out. And guess what? In about six months, all of my toes were looking beautiful again.

What happened to my toes and the remedy is a picture of what happens to all of us. Our past must be healed by the blood of Jesus working its way from the inside of us and eventually showing up on the outside in our behavior, countenance, decisions and lifestyle. It is only through an internal work that you can truly be healed and set free from the experiences of your past. There is no job, no spouse, no outfit and no cosmetic surgery that can replace what only God can do to heal you inside.

A verse in Romans makes the same statement: "Do not conform yourselves to the standards of this world, but let God transform you inwardly by a complete change of your mind. Then you will be able to know the will of God" (Rom. 12:2, *TEV*). God always works from the inside out. Satan works just the opposite; he works from the outside in. He works to destroy your life through outward temptations and struggles that only eat away at you on the inside.

Many times, we hide unresolved issues from our past under a multitude of disguises. We try to overcome rejection and insecurity by losing weight, working out, dressing cute and appearing confident. We hide pain under a smile. We say we've forgiven someone for the hurt they caused in our life, but we vow to never get that close to anyone again. We cover our shame by a series of church activities to hopefully earn God's love.

As long as we're suppressing things from our past, the "infection" or "wound" of what happened to us is killing us inside. It doesn't matter what happens outwardly in our life; nothing will truly make us happy and fulfilled until we allow God to completely get our junk out of us.

Right now you may be reading this book and not even realize there is something inside of you that must be uprooted and dealt with, because it's "polished over." Or you may be reading this book because you've reached a desperate point in your life and you're looking for answers, hope and help. You know *something* or *someone* is keeping you back from being all God wants you to be.

It's important that you realize you cannot change anything. You cannot change what happened. You cannot change how you acted. You cannot change yesterday. You cannot even change yourself. But God can. God can change every hurt in your life into a testimony for someone else. He can take every tear you've ever shed and replace it with hope, purpose and vision for your life! He is known for turning sadness into joy and making beauty out of ashes!

So, how do you begin the healing process within? It takes effect the moment you repent. You need to examine your life, look deep inside and say, "God, I know that what I did was not pleasing to You." It may be big or it may be small, but to God, sin is sin. It's vital that you repent of anything and everything that could be keeping you from experiencing the peace of God. Whatever it is, get it out.

The apostle Paul tells us, "Repent ye therefore, and be converted, that your sins may be blotted out, when the times of refreshing shall come from the presence of the Lord" (Acts 3:19, KJV). Do you want to experience the presence of the Lord? Would you like to be refreshed? According to this verse, repentance is the key to experiencing that presence and that refreshing.

Let's look at a man who was the pictorial definition for true repentance. The psalmist David was referred to as a man after God's own heart (see 1 Sam. 13:14), yet he was a man who committed adultery and murder. How in the world could God refer to him with such loving words? Because David repented. He got his heart right before God. He emptied himself of every single thing that was keeping him weighted down and miserable inside. He knew he couldn't go forward in life until he brought all of his shame, guilt and sin before God in the light. Listen to what David had to say before he repented:

BLESSED (HAPPY, fortunate, to be envied) is he who has forgiveness of his transgression continually exercised upon him, whose sin is covered.

Blessed (happy, fortunate, to be envied) is the man to whom the Lord imputes no iniquity and in whose spirit there is no deceit.

When I kept silence [before I confessed], my bones wasted away through my groaning all the day long.

For day and night Your hand [of displeasure] was heavy upon me; my moisture was turned into the drought of summer. . . .

I acknowledged my sin to You, and my iniquity I did not hide. I said, I will confess my transgressions to the Lord [continually *unfolding the past till all is told*]—then You [instantly] forgave me the *guilt and iniquity* of my sin (Ps. 32:1-5, *AMP*).

David was referring to a lot of pain inside. David probably appeared fine on the outside to everyone else, but his hidden sin was eating away at him on the inside. When he kept silent, he stayed miserable. When he kept silent, he stayed tormented. When he kept silent, he stayed where he was. You may look fine on the outside, but what is going on inside of you? Why are you keeping silent before God, when all you have to do is get it out? Get it out in the open between you and God, and empty yourself in His presence.

The word "repent" means a "change of mind." It means to turn your back, walk away and make a decision not to commit that same sin again. It means getting your thinking in line with God's. It means asking God to forgive you for something you've done wrong. It means walking away from your old lifestyle. "Everything—and I do mean everything—connected to that old way of life has to go. . . . Get rid of it! And then take on an entirely new way of life—a God-fashioned life, a life renewed from the inside and working itself into your conduct as God accurately reproduces his character in you . . . Make a clean break" (Eph. 4:22-24,31, *THE MESSAGE*).

Just like we discussed in chapter 2, set aside a time to be alone with God and open up to Him. Tell Him everything. He already knows what you're hiding anyway. Get everything out in the open once and for all so that you never have to think about it or talk about it ever again. You have to be emptied out in order for God to fill you up with His love. Repentance is a two-way street. It's an emptying out and a filling up. Empty out the hurts, the scars, the wounds, the junk; and let God fill you up with peace like you've never known before, joy unspeakable and vision for a new life. "Let us strip off every weight that slows us down, especially the sin that so easily trips us up" (Heb. 12:1, *NLT*). Once you set that time aside to do nothing but repent and receive God's amazing love for you, you need to take an active step in forgiving yourself.

Step 2: Forgive Yourself!

This has been the hardest step for me. In most cases, because I grew up in church and should have "known better," it's been extremely challenging to forgive myself. If you have a Type A personality or you're always wanting to please others, it can be the fight of your life to admit that you don't measure up to your own expectations.

Even so, God's forgiveness is available and immediate. Psalm 32:5 says, "You [instantly] forgave me the guilt and iniquity of my sin" (*AMP*). God *instantly* forgives. You don't have to wait two years before God wipes your slate clean. It happens immediately. God doesn't just forgive what you've done and then leave you with the guilt. He is such an amazing God. He knew that Satan would be doing his best to consume us with guilt even after we repent, so God mentioned it in His Word. He wants you totally free from everything connected to your past.

Guilt can be defined as "the state of a moral agent that results from his actual commission of a crime or offense, knowing it to be a crime, or violation of law. . . . The guilt of a person exists, *as soon as* the crime is committed. . . . Guilt renders a person a debtor to the law, as it binds him to *pay a penalty* in money or *suffering*. Guilt therefore implies both criminality and liableness to punishment."[1]

Wow! Satan definitely wants you to pay the penalty for your sins through much suffering. He'll do it any way you let him. It may be a feeling of worthlessness, guilt, insecurity, bitterness or rejection. Satan will use whatever has held you back your entire life to keep you down.

Satan can destroy you with guilt. He knows that if the "sin" or the "offense" that was done to you doesn't destroy you, then a guilty conscience will. His plan is to keep you so down on yourself that you will never do what God has called you to do, because you feel such shame. "Guilt" actually means "to press down." That's why Jesus is called the lifter of our heads (see Ps. 3:3).

Isn't that amazing? Satan came to press you down, depress you, discourage you and cause you to carry yourself with your head down in shame. Jesus came to give you a new life, a new identity and a new vision to lift your head in confidence.

In Romans 8:1, Paul reminds us, "There is therefore now no condemnation to those who are in Christ Jesus, who do not walk according to the flesh, but according to the Spirit" (*NKJV*). If you don't forgive yourself, what you are really saying is that the blood of Jesus didn't work. But it did work. Jesus carried the very sin that you're still holding in your heart to the cross. He carried it for you. His blood washed your sins away. When you repent of your sin, it is gone. It's not on your record.

Isn't It Time You Forgave Yourself?

You will *never* stop hurting until you forgive yourself. You need to see yourself the way God sees you. He doesn't see sin; He sees forgiveness. He sees His love for you. He sees His plan and reason for your birth. God doesn't even remember your sins once you've repented (see Heb. 10:16-18). He won't even bring them up ever again. Satan will keep bringing them up, and even other people will. But rest assured, God never will.

Satan will always base your identity on your past experiences. He even did it with Jesus, and Jesus was perfect. Jesus never sinned, but when He was in the wilderness, fasting for 40 days, Satan was there, waiting to tempt Him. He taunted, "*If* you're the son of God . . ." He knew full well who Jesus was. He'd known it since the beginning of time. So why did he repeatedly say, "If you're the Son of God" to Jesus? Because he wanted Jesus to question His own identity.

You'd better believe the devil will do the same to you. He wants you to be defined as the girl who had the abortion; the girl who slept around; the guy who smokes pot; the adulterer; the hypocrite; the alcoholic; the druggie; the loser. Why? Because shame is his game. He knows that shame and guilt will keep you from your future. Well, his plan didn't work with Jesus, and it doesn't have to work in your life either.

Every time Satan said, "If you're the son of God . . ." Jesus combatted him by speaking the Word of God. He would audibly declare, "It is written . . ." and confess the Word. That very same strategy can work for you. Every time Satan brings up your past, you have to get to a point that you speak the Word of God back to him. That's how you shut him up!

Believe What God's Word Says About You

There are two keys to forgiving yourself. First, you must believe God's Word more than you believe how you feel. As I mentioned earlier, you may never "feel" righteous or in right standing with God. You can't live by what you think about yourself or how you feel about yourself.

You have to choose to live by what you know the Word of God says about you. What does it say? "Therefore, if anyone is in Christ, he is a new creation; old things have passed away; behold, all things have become new" (2 Cor. 5:17, *NKJV*).

If you're a new creation, you have no past. It reminds me of my little nephew, Bryn, who is still a toddler. When we were in the hospital seeing Bryn for the first time after he was born, we didn't say, "Oh, look how tiny he is. Look at his little chin like his daddy's, and his mother's eyes. Oh, he's so cute, but . . . oh, my goodness, look at his past." Of course not. Bryn doesn't have a past! He's brand new. He's done nothing wrong. He's innocent. Well, so are you the moment you repent. Now, that doesn't mean you won't ever make mistakes after repentance. You will. We all do. Just keep repenting.

Accepting God's righteousness is not based on your feelings. It's based on the Word of God and the price Jesus paid on the cross. It's a simple acceptance of that gift that will lead you toward total forgiveness. It will also give you the self-esteem and confidence to do what God has called you to do.

Speak What God's Word Says Is True

Second, you must say what you believe, not what you feel. You must declare on a daily basis, "I believe that I am the righteousness of God in Christ Jesus." What that means is that you are in right standing with God not because of what you've done but because of what Jesus has done for you. Confess that daily until it sinks in!

Speaking the Word of God out of your mouth is the most powerful weapon you have for defeating the devil. In Ephesians 6:17, Paul says that the weapon we are to wield in our battle against Satan is the Sword of the Spirit, which is the Word of God. Revelation 12:11 says that we overcome Satan through the word of our testimony: "They overcame him by the blood of the Lamb and by the word of their testimony" (Rev. 12:11, *KJV*). When I caught hold of this tactic of warfare, I made it a point to consciously speak out against the very thing that Satan uses to torment me. If he tries to intimidate me with fear, I start saying, "Father, I thank You that Your Word says, 'Fear not! There is nothing to fear!'" If the devil tries to remind me of my past, I declare, "Thank You, Lord, that Your Word says that I am the righteousness of God in Christ Jesus. Thank You, Jesus, for washing my sins away and making me right with God."

Step 3: Forgive Others

Unforgiveness can be deadly! Think for a moment about Jesus on the cross. He had never sinned in His life; yet He was beaten, spit on, abused, lied about, humiliated, rejected, laughed at and, ultimately, killed. But what did He say on the cross?

Father, forgive them; for they know not what they do (Luke 23:34, *KJV*).

Wow! Those are powerful words. This just shows the extent of His love for humanity. Jesus didn't say something to justify His actions and prove who He really was. What He said proved His love for people through the act of forgiving. You might be thinking, *Okay, that's great that Jesus did that. But you don't know what I've been through. I can't forgive. I'm not Jesus Christ.*

I would never belittle what you've been through, and I don't minimize the pain you've experienced. I am, however, very aware that harboring unforgiveness in your heart against others is a weapon that Satan can use to destroy your life. The apostle Paul said that forgiveness shuts the door to Satan's schemes against us: "I have forgiven in the sight of Christ for your sake, in order that Satan might not outwit us. For we are not unaware of his schemes" (2 Cor. 2:10-11).

I would never say that it's easy to forgive. The truth is that sometimes it can be the hardest thing to do. But it is *necessary* if you want to be healed from the hurts that are accumulating in your life. If you can't forgive, you can't live a peaceful life ... ever. Jesus warned us clearly in Matthew 6:14-15 that if we forgive others when they sin against us, our heavenly Father will also forgive us; but if we do not forgive others, then our Father will not forgive us. Unforgiveness will build up in your heart and eat away at you like a cancer. It will get bigger and bigger, especially the more you dwell on it and the more you tell others about how badly you've been mistreated. It will paralyze you from moving forward.

Have you ever used a magnifying glass? You know that when you place it on top of an object, the object increases in size. Everything around it seems to fade into oblivion and only the object is visible. When you repeatedly talk about what someone has done to you with your friends, your family and your coworkers, you are magnifying that grievance so that it becomes the biggest thing in your life. It drowns out any potential around you for something greater.

I know someone who consistently talks about the pain of her past every time you're around her. While the experience happened 15 years ago, she brings it up day after day. She is reliving it every time she tells another person how badly she was treated. The pain of reminding herself of what happened is keeping her from moving forward in her life.

In my teenage years, I was severely hurt by people who probably haven't even given me a second thought. I went through a very traumatic experience as a young girl with one guy in particular and was left to feel worthless, ugly, unwanted and rejected. Has he ever called and apologized? Has he ever seen me in the media and felt convicted? Has he ever written to me and asked for forgiveness? Are you kidding? He probably doesn't even remember what happened! Most of the people who have hurt you aren't thinking about what happened. They've moved on. Now it's your turn.

The people who caused us pain are not the enemy. The enemy is Satan. He is the one behind every touch of evil in your life. Please remember that! Don't allow that person to keep you from your destiny. Why would you want anyone to have the power to destroy your future?

So how do you forgive someone who has hurt you? By faith! It's not something you feel (just like accepting forgiveness); it's something you do. You choose to forgive.

As I shared with you earlier, my husband and I went through severe marriage difficulties, and we separated for a season. We had many unresolved issues from our past and as a result of getting married the way we did. During that time, I was full of mixed emotions, pain, anger and unforgiveness. I was hurting so badly inside about everything, including my own bad choices and bad attitudes, and I had no compassion for my husband. I flat out didn't want to be married anymore, and I had become very calloused inside. I was reminded of the verse that states, "Forgive, and you will be forgiven" (Luke 6:37, *NIV*). I knew that I needed to forgive him if I ever wanted God to forgive me. And I needed God's forgiveness in a big way. I realized that forgiveness was a choice that absolutely had to be made. There was no room for excuses, but the truth was, I didn't want to.

I remember one particular moment like it was yesterday. I picked up a photo of Rodney and me, and I covered his face with my hand (I didn't even want to look at him). I then began praying in the Spirit, walking around in circles in my den and kitchen. It was step one in forgiving. I couldn't even pray in English! Believe me, praying in your heavenly language does wonders for bringing peace in a tumultuous situation.

I did the same thing every morning. I would make myself pray over that photo. Gradually, I began to move my hand and look at Rodney and pray in the Spirit. Finally, I could actually say, "In the name of Jesus, I choose—as an act of my faith—to forgive my husband. And I choose to forgive myself." That's all I was able to say, but I knew it was what had to be done.

My dad tells a story about a woman who was in the hospital dying from cancer. Her husband called our office and asked if my dad would fly up to where they lived and pray for her. Dad flew up there, and when he was in the hospital room, he quietly asked the Lord if there was anything specific he should pray over her or encourage her. He heard the Lord say, "Tell her that if she'll forgive her husband, she can be healed."

Apparently, this woman's husband had been involved in an affair years ago, and she was not able to let go of that pain. My dad gently whispered to her, "The Lord just told me to tell you that if you'll forgive your husband, you can be healed of this cancer." Without hesitation, she said, "I will never forgive him." She died soon afterward.

Unforgiveness does not kill the person who hurt you; it kills you. It kills your potential. It kills your future. I heard Stormie Omartian say that forgiving the person who hurt you does not make that person right; it makes you free! I have firsthand experience that this is true. As I began praying over the photo of my husband, and I prayed this way every single day, I began to gradually change. In time, my anger turned to compassion. It didn't happen overnight. It didn't happen over the next week or even the next month. But it happened. I quit telling the story of my pain.

I quit thinking about it. I quit dwelling on it. I began to dwell on God, more than I dwelt on my problems, until I was eventually healed and so was my marriage.

I know it's hard. It's not easy to forgive. But if you want to live out God's best . . . if you ever want to experience peace and joy in

your life . . . if you want to be the recipient of God's divine healing, you must forgive. Do you want to stop hurting? Forgiveness
is the answer.

Note

1. *Noah Webster's 1828 American Dictionary,* s.v. "guilt." http://www.1828-dictionary.com/d/
search/word,guilt.

4

WHEN YOU HAVE A PLAN... *YOU WON'T LOOK BACK*

I want to share a simple solution with you that has become the most profound key in turning my life around. When my marriage was on the brink of divorce, and I began seeing a marriage counselor, Dr. Farmer recognized tremendous fear in my life. He told me five little words that have changed the way I confront my fears. He said, "Fight fear with a plan."

Fight Fear with a Plan!

Acting on those five words has not only catapulted me out of my past, but it has also truly enabled me to walk right into my destiny! It can do the same for you.

It was during this painful time that I had no vision or goals for my life. Dr. Farmer helped me see that I needed a daily plan that included goals surrounding the most important areas of my life. If I wanted to get through my storm, I would have to incorporate goal planning and execute the plan in my daily routine.

Writing down a list of goals is a habit that successful people live by. Having a plan is what gets your eyes off the past and into the present and future. Cosmetic genius Mary Kay Ash is the founder of a beauty line that reached $2.4 billion in wholesale sales in the United States alone. She attributed her success to the fact that every day she wrote down six of the most important things to do each day.

There is a saying that *the secret of your future is hidden in your daily routine*. This was something Mary Kay Ash knew. This was something Dr. Farmer advocated. And this was something I was going to have to learn. I believe that changes need to be made on a regular basis in order to experience freedom from the past. Nothing happens overnight. You have to prepare for a successful future. You have to formulate a plan. You have to put it into action. Only then will you walk into a future that is full of purpose.

In my case, after Dr. Farmer mentioned to me the importance of writing down goals, I took some time to think about what some of the most important things in my life were. I didn't want to waste another miserable moment stuck going nowhere, so I hit the ground running. I made a list of things I'd like to share with you in detail so that you can see how a plan is created and executed.

Here are four guidelines to remember as you start thinking about your own goals.

1. *Goals must be in writing.* "Goals that are not written down are just wishes."[1] Even God tells us the importance of putting things down on paper. Habakkuk reminds us to write the vision (see Hab. 2:2).

2. *Goals must be measurable.* There's a big difference in saying, "I want to lose weight" and saying "I will lose 10 pounds by March 1." Your goals must be measured by something; this is what increases your chances of achieving them.

3. *Goals must be realistic.* If your goals are completely unrealistic, then you're setting yourself up for defeat. If your goal is to get closer to God, then you need to be realistic

in how you plan to get closer to God. Don't tell yourself you will pray for four hours every day. Be practical. Set aside 30 minutes of alone time a day instead. It's important to set realistic and attainable goals so that you are able to reach them.

4. *Goals must have a deadline.* Isn't it amazing how a deadline causes us to work harder? When my sister and I were younger, and we were told to unload the dishwasher, we would look at the clock and see how fast we could get it done, in less than four minutes. We were determined to reach our goal. Why? We had a deadline. It's been said that the most productive time in an office is the day before vacation. Why? There's a deadline. People get more done in that one day than they do in a week! Always assign a deadline to your goals. It's energizing and motivating.

Also, when you're setting goals for yourself, you need to answer the following four questions, which will help guide you through the overall purpose for what you want to achieve. Your answers will build the framework of your plan and put it into action.

1. *What* am I doing?
2. *Why* am I doing this?
3. *How* am I going to do this?
4. *When* am I going to do this?

Let's get back to my assignment. Here are the six things I wanted to focus on every single day. I'm going to walk you through the process I went through in formulating this plan. Use my example as a reference for yours.

1. Faith (my relationship with God)
2. Family (my home life)
3. Finances (my income and expenses)
4. Fitness (my health and wellbeing)
5. Friendships (my time with those closest to me)
6. Free time (time for myself)

Goal 1: My Faith

Knowing that faith is the foundation of my life, I knew that I had to get closer to God. In order to do this, I was focused on hearing the Word. It has been proven that it takes 21 days to break an old habit and start a new one. My plan was to commit to studying the Word for that period of time to build my faith and create that new discipline in my life. Why did I do that? Because the Bible says, "For whatever is born of God overcomes the world. And this is the victory that has overcome the world—our faith" (1 John 5:4, *NKJV*).

It takes faith to overcome defeat. It takes faith to overcome addictions. It takes faith to overcome depression. It takes faith to overcome hopelessness. It takes faith to overcome sickness, laziness, procrastination and painful memories of the past.

"So then faith comes by hearing, and hearing by the word of God" (Rom. 10:17, *NKJV*). I like to think that faith comes from hearing and hearing and hearing and hearing the Word of God. In other words, you never stop! It's a habit like brushing your teeth. You could say, "I've brushed my teeth 300,000 times now; can I stop?" Well, you could. But one, it's gross; and two, your teeth will eventually rot. I knew that I needed to build my faith because I needed to overcome things in my life. I invested in faith-building sermons I could listen to in my CD player.

I looked around my house and realized I didn't have many. So I took a trip to my mom and dad's house and borrowed a bunch of CDs and tapes from their massive collection. I visited the websites of my favorite preachers and made myself purchase some new, fresh material that was relevant to my situation. I could hardly wait for them to arrive in the mail.

I also had a plan to take it to the next level. I had to be realistic in *when* I was going to do *what* I had to do. I also had to ask myself, "*When* am I realistically going to make time to listen to these messages?" When you are planning time to spend with God, you must be practical about it. Really study your schedule. It's probably not realistic to listen to the Word at work, or when you are putting the kids to bed, or when you are ready to go to sleep. For me, I had to find time in the morning, while I was getting ready for work. When is the best time for you? It can be when you're doing laundry, when you are going for your morning walk or when you have your mid-afternoon cup of coffee.

After 21 days of listening to God's Word, there was a profound change that took place in my spirit. I was not the same woman I was when I began that goal. Remember, God works from the inside out. You won't necessarily "see" the changes, but you will be changing every single time you hear the Word. Don't ever think that it's a waste of time. Just study and hear the Word and you will notice a difference.

Here's how I answered the four questions surrounding my faith goal:

1. *What* am I going to do? Pursue God in some way every day.
2. *Why* am I doing this? In order to build a stronger relationship with Him (because I know He is my only answer).
3. *How* am I going to do this? By spending 10 minutes every morning in prayer (worshiping Him, singing songs of praise, speaking faith-filled Scriptures out of my mouth, talking with Him about everything).
4. *When* am I going to do this? I will set aside 10 minutes every morning before I get dressed for the day (from 6:50 to 7:00 A.M.).

It's really that simple.

Goal 2: My Family

I wanted to have a peaceful home even though my life wasn't at peace. A peaceful home, in the midst of tumultuous circumstances, meant to me that I would not let my daughter, Kassidi, see me crying; I would not talk to others about my situation if she were around; and in particular it meant that my home would be clean and organized. Those things were my pathway to peace.

I didn't realize how therapeutic this entire process was, but it proved to provide more emotional healing than I ever could have imagined. I began writing a daily vision for one room in our house at a time. Each day, one particular room was cleaned out, organized and sprayed with air freshener.

As I cleaned each room, I listened to the Word. I carried my CD player with me and listened to message after message as I opened every cabinet, cleaned out every drawer and wiped off every countertop. My tormented mind was focused on a cleaning project *and* hearing the life-changing Word of God at the same time.

When you are hearing the Word, it's not like just listening to music or hearing background noise. It is changing you because it is getting down inside of you. Every time you hear the Word, your spirit is being recharged. It is being fed, and it is getting stronger. The stronger your spirit gets, the weaker your flesh will become.

Here's how I answered the four questions surrounding my family goal:

1. *What* am I going to do? Clean and organize every room in my house and listen to God's Word while I'm cleaning.
2. *Why* am I doing this? To provide a peaceful atmosphere at home.
3. *How* am I going to do this? By starting with one room at a time and then cleaning out every drawer, cabinet and closet.
4. *When* am I going to do this? Saturday mornings at 9:00 A.M.

Goal 3: My Finances

As I sat in my study thinking about these six areas in my life that I needed to focus on, I had to take a hard look at my finances. My income had drastically changed, and I needed a plan.

It's going to take finances to do whatever God has called you to do, and if you spend everything you make, then you're not going to get very far. Obviously, this book is more about emotional healing than financial planning, and I don't plan to spend many pages writing about how to get your finances in order. But I will suggest setting a goal as it relates to this aspect of your life. There are great books in print by intelligent and well-experienced financial planners that you should purchase to help you in this area. It's an important area to manage in your life in order to get to the place where God wants you to be, specifically, free from financial burdens.

I know many people who have no financial plan. They don't have a budget in place, and so they don't save money, they don't tithe, their bills are piling up and they are slaves to their financial condition. Consequently, they live in constant fear.

If you make $50,000 a year but you spend $50,000 a year, what will you have at the end of the year? Nothing. If you do the same thing for the next 10 years, what will you have? Nothing. Do you think that's what God wants for your life? Of course not.

Here are three tips to take control of your finances today:

1. Pay your tithe (10 percent of your income belongs to God).
2. Pay yourself (set a goal to save 10 percent).
3. Pay your bills (set a goal to live on 80 percent).

If you're not tithing right now, don't go another day without committing to this goal. The first step toward a major turnaround in your finances is to tithe. It is an act of love to God, and it is sowing seed rather than something you owe Him. "'Bring all the tithes into the storehouse, that there may be food in My house, and try me now in this,' says the LORD of hosts, 'if I will not open for you the windows of heaven and pour out for you such blessing that there will not be room enough to receive it'" (Mal. 3:10, *NKJV*).

It's a good idea to set some financial goals in giving to the Lord. Let's say you would like to give $1,200 to the Lord's work this year through your church and other ministries that you believe in. Break that goal down into measurable steps. Giving $1,200 for the year breaks into $100 each month, which means around $25 each week. Now that's attainable. See, it isn't so hard!

Paying yourself involves saving money. Look at what you can save, and then set a goal for the year. How much do you want to have in your savings by the end of the year or by next year? Is it written down? Is it measurable? Is it realistic? Does it have a deadline?

If you can put $10 aside from every paycheck, that's a start. You may not think it's much, but over time it will add up. And, hey, if you're not saving money at all, then you'll be miles ahead of where you are now. Look for ways to put something in your savings account from every pay period. Sacrifice one meal of eating out so you can fulfill your goal of putting $10, $20, $50 into your savings.

Get into a habit of thinking about your savings account with every bit of income you receive. If it's birthday money, a bonus check, profits from a garage sale or however you obtain extra money, put something in your savings. It will invigorate you in preparing toward your future.

If you're in debt, which 61 percent of Americans are, then get a plan to get out of debt. Do extra things to earn income. Babysit for someone. Clean someone's house. Sell things online. Sell your old books and VHS movies that you don't watch anymore. Don't give up. Don't think that you're so far gone that it doesn't matter to rack up a few more bills! Get control of your past spending by setting some goals for today. Many financial experts recommend paying off your smallest bill first. Write down all of your debt and determine which is the smallest bill. Then slowly pay off one at a time, applying the payment you used to apply to the now paid-off debt to the next debt in line. And shred your old credit cards. Don't rack up new debt!

Remember, your goal is to get your eyes off of your past and onto your future. "A person with no vision (for their finances) will always return to their past."

1. *What* am I going to do? Save $500 within 12 months.
2. *Why* am I doing this? To be in control of my finances and have an emergency fund.
3. *How* am I going to do this? Resist eating out one day a week, thus saving $10 each week.
4. *When* am I going to do this? This week—I will take lunch to work with me on Tuesday.

It's really that simple. You just need a plan.

Goal 4: Fitness

I read something the other day that made me laugh: "I signed up for an exercise class. It said, 'Wear loose-fitting clothing.' If I had any loose-fitting clothing, I wouldn't have signed up in the first place!"

There is a correlation between emotional health and physical health. If you're filled with all sorts of wounds and memories of the past, one of the best ways to support your goals toward freedom and being made whole is to physically take charge of your life. Studies have shown that people feel better when they exercise. And many look better as well!

If you don't spend time working out, I suggest making a plan to do so. Be realistic about it. If you have not worked out your entire life, don't expect to train for a marathon in one week. Start slow. Take your time. Do what works for you. Maybe it's walking; maybe it's running, swimming, taking an aerobics class or cycling. Just get your heart pumping for 30 minutes a day and you'll notice quite a difference!

I'm a junk-food junkie. I love my sweets. So in my case, I've had to cut down on those things and eat more vegetables and fruits. I started slowly. I began drinking more water every day, limited myself on snacks and gradually increased my exercise. It took awhile for me to get into a routine, but because I took my time with it, these great habits have lasted to this day.

I don't know what works for you as far as fitness, but I know that maintaining good overall health is vital to our wellbeing. Go to your local bookstore and buy books on health, nutrition and fitness. Make a plan for your life that includes being fit, and stick with it. Get a personal trainer if you need to. Find a friend who will work out with you. Write down your goals and progress in an exercise journal and track your results!

I love walking, and I highly recommend it. When I walk, I pray and worship God; so not only does it increase my fitness level, but it also strengthens my spiritual walk (no pun intended). I encourage you to walk a little bit every day. Put on your sneakers, go outside and get some fresh air, and spend time with God as your body indulges in a workout.

God is a great workout partner. My walks with Him have healed so much in me. I do most of the talking, but it's still therapeutic. I know I'm not just talking to the sky. I know that He hears every single word I say. I've spent my time walking, crying and praying; and by the end of every walk, I've felt refreshed, renewed and filled with incredible peace.

I really want to encourage you to start small—to start where you are and then build on it. Set a goal to walk for 15 minutes a day. But here's the key: be consistent about those 15 minutes a day. Don't stop! It only takes one diet to lose weight. Which diet? The one you stick with! Consistency is the key to change in every area of life.

One more key: I've recognized in my own life that the best way to start a new habit is to do something at the same time every day. For instance, when I take my vitamins, I do it every single morning before I walk out the door to exercise. I don't even have to remind myself to take them because it's just part of my routine.

Start a habit of doing something to feel better about yourself phys-ically—and do it consistently. Pursue the new you!

1. *What* am I going to do? Exercise.
2. *Why* am I doing this? To lose 10 pounds.
3. *How* am I going to do this? Eat better and walk outside five times a week.
4. *When* am I going to do this? Every weekday morning from 5:00 to 6:00 A.M.

Goal 5: Friendships

Who you hang around has everything to do with how you are going to act. If you want to see where your life is headed, look at the list of names in your cell phone. It is very important that you look for peo-ple you admire. Search out those people who have qualities that you would like to have. Ask them out to lunch, and learn from them. Spend time with people who lift you up rather than bring you down.

If you don't know anyone like that, then read books by people you admire and respect. Listen to their messages on CD. Learn everything you can from them. It will change your life. A friend of mine, Erik Lawson, said one time when a bunch of us were out to dinner, "I have spent time with Michael Jordan, Donald Trump, Joyce Meyer and John Maxwell." The rest of us sat there with our mouths open in envy until he said, "But I've never met any one of them." We were confused. What was he talking about? He laughed and said, "I spend time learning from them when I'm driving back and forth to work, listening to them on CD for 20 minutes every day;

and I've read all their books." What a great lesson for us to follow!

Friendships are vital in holding you accountable in not returning to your past. I have two really close accountability partners, my best friends, who know some of the temptations I've dealt with in my past. I know they will not let me go back to that awful place! I know, without a doubt in my mind, that God used my best friend during a very vulnerable time in my life when Satan was tempting me.

If Theresa hadn't been so bold and in my face about what was happening, I do not believe you would be reading this book today. In fact, I frequently tell her that she will receive credit for every life that is helped through my ministry. Scripture tells us, "A man who isolates himself seeks his own desire; he rages against all wise judgment" (Prov. 18:1, *NKJV*).

Like me, you might have a tendency to isolate yourself from people when you're going through a tough time. Keep in mind that Satan likes to keep you isolated. He knows where you're weak, and he knows how to play on your emotions. If you keep godly counsel around you, they can keep you strong. They can help you stay focused on reaching your new goals and keep you walking toward your new life.

1. *What* am I going to do? Pursue friendships with people I respect and enjoy.
2. *Why* am I doing this? To stay strong in my faith and stay accountable so I won't give in to sin.
3. *How* am I going to do this? Plan get-togethers twice a month.
4. *When* am I going to do this? Saturdays at 6:00 P.M.

Goal 6: Free Time

"Plan my free time? You've got to be kidding me!" No, I'm serious. When you're in a mental battle to either go backward to your old thoughts, memories and ways of doing things, you can't give Satan *any* territory or he will come barging in and take full advantage of your life. I'm not saying you have to be busy or active 24 hours a day, 7 days a week. I am saying you have to plan each day on purpose.

Do whatever you need to do to quit concentrating on the past. If your plan is to rest, then rest; and don't feel guilty about it. Do things that you have always wanted to do but never got around to it because you were weighed down by old memories. Take up that hobby. Rekindle an old friendship. Volunteer for that organization. Get a part-time job. Take music lessons. It doesn't matter what you do as long as it's healthy and it keeps you away from the past.

I like to suggest writing a list of the things you want to do before you die. It doesn't matter how many items are on that list or how impossible they may seem. Write them down.

I read about a man who was featured in a national magazine article because he made a list of all the things he wanted to do.[2] He had been inspired to do this by his grandmother who would constantly say, "I wish I had done that when I was younger." This man thought to himself that he would never say that when he got older. So, he began writing his list, which included things like:

- Ride a horse in the Rose Bowl Parade
- Read the entire *Encyclopedia Britannica*
- Be a missionary in church

- Trace the travels of Marco Polo
- Read the writings of Shakespeare

He was 15 years old when he wrote this list, which included 127 tasks. By the end of his life, he had accomplished 108 of the 127 things he set out to do! Many of us have not accomplished one thing we wanted to do. Many of us haven't even gotten started by making such a list! Can you finally see the importance of writing down goals and visions on paper? Those who write their goals accomplish significantly more than those who do not.[3]

1. *What* am I going to do? Make a list of everything I want to do before I die.
2. *Why* am I doing this? So I can see my dreams on paper and live my life with purpose.
3. *How* am I going to do this? Take time to really think of all the places I'd like to see and things I'd like to experience, and write them down.
4. *When* am I going to do this? Sunday evening I will get started, and I'll keep adding to my list.

Warning: Satan does not want you to have any goals on paper. He wants to control your life by controlling your dreams. He doesn't want you to have any dreams, for that matter; he wants you to live in the past, remember? So, shut him up by writing down your goals and pursue them with faith and passion. There is a popular saying: Men decide their habits; their habits decide their future. When you make a habit of focusing on the things you want to accomplish and spend your energy on things that will build up your faith and your emotional, physical and mental wellbeing, it will lead you straight into God's perfect plan for your life.

Why? Because the secret of your future is hidden in your daily routine. It's what you do every single day that matters. If you are reading this chapter and thinking, *Terri, I've done all this stuff before and nothing has changed,* my advice to you is this: It's not that you haven't done the right thing before; you probably just haven't done it long enough to see lasting change. Consistency is the key to change in every area of your life. Don't just think in terms of goals; think habits! You can do it; you just need to get started. Speaker and author Lee J. Colan says, "You don't have to be great to get started, but you do have to get started to be great."[4]

Notes
1. Cited in Gary Ryan Blair, *Goals: Guidelines for Designing an Extraordinary Life* (Aurora, IL: Successories, Inc., 1999).
2. John Goddard, "Another Check Mark on the List," quoted in Jack Canfield and Mark Victor Hansen, *Chicken Soup for the Soul* (Deerfield Beach, FL: Health Communications, Inc., 1993), p. 185.
3. Gail Matthews, Ph.D, "Brief Summary of Recent Goals Research," Dominican University of California, http://www.dominican.edu/academics/ahss/psych/faculty/fulltime/gail matthews.html.
4. Lee J. Colan, *Sticking to It: The Art of Adherence* (Dallas, TX: Cornerstone Leadership Institute, 2003).

5

WHEN THE MEMORIES WON'T GO AWAY... *YOU HAVE TO GET AGGRESSIVE*

An 83-year-old grandmother lay dying on a hospital bed. As pale as a ghost and hooked up to IVs, the woman sighed and painfully remarked, "I've been a bad little girl." Though barely a whisper, the nurses overheard their patient's mournful voice cry these words out repeatedly for the last three weeks of her life. They never knew why she said it, but it broke their hearts to hear her.

The elderly woman, who had thinning gray hair and deep wrinkles, and did not even recognize her own son, was tormented by memories she had never forgotten. She had gotten pregnant out of wedlock as a young girl. Six decades later, she was still tormented by the agony of what she went through. This woman, at the age of 83, still defined herself by her past. She was not only the daughter of a preacher; she was also my great-grandmother. Her name was Vena Savelle.

The Power of the Past

Every person you come in contact with has a past. Every person has memories of things they did or said or witnessed that they simply wish weren't there. The power of the past is no respecter of persons, backgrounds, gender, age or race. Therapists and counselors around the world are filling up their appointment books every day with people who still hold on to their past—old men and young men, old women and young women, teenagers, children. Many counseling sessions begin with the question: "So what happened?" What do we all want? To deal with and get over our past! If the past is still being relived *in your mind*, it becomes your present and ultimately destroys any chance of you experiencing a purposeful future.

You can witness this in the story I mentioned about my great-grandmother. She thought about what happened to her for more than 60 years. She replayed, rehearsed and revisited this event over and over until that's all she became. Vena Savelle became her past.

You know by now that I, too, have been plagued by the memories of the past. Past experiences. Past decisions. Past relationships. Past hurts. Past disappointments. Past guilt. Past shame. It seems that no matter how much time has gone by, if I allow my mind to stroll down memory lane, the pain surfaces instantly. There have been many times when I have walked into my closet, leaned my head against the wall and cried out for God to erase the memories. There have been many times when I have driven past a part of town that instantly takes me to a hurtful place and makes my heart ache. I have spent countless nights lying in my bed staring into the dark, remembering . . . and hurting.

Why, Lord, why can't You just erase the past?

I can't tell you how many times I've heard a minister say, "get over your past" and then quickly move on to their next point. It has been very frustrating. I'd sit there and think, *Wait a minute! Back up, please! You're not telling me how to get over my past, and I need to know how!* My lack of knowledge just amped up my mental anguish even more, and I was left to wonder things like, *What is wrong with me? How come everyone else can get over their past? How can my past get fixed? Will this pain ever go away?*

Oh, how the devil loves to see you thinking these thoughts! He wants you to feel crazy, weak, pathetic and useless. He'll put thoughts in your head to feed your feelings. Thankfully, you are not alone. The devil likes to torment all of us, and God gave us a warning about it in His Word:

Resist him, standing firm in the faith, because you know that your brothers throughout the world are undergoing the *same* kind of sufferings (1 Pet. 5:9, *NIV*, emphasis added).

Keep a cool head. Stay alert. The Devil is poised to pounce, and would like nothing better than to catch you napping. Keep your guard up. You're not *the only ones* plunged into these hard times (1 Pet. 5:8-9, *THE MESSAGE*, emphasis added).

Satan uses all sorts of tactics to torment you. He can even use something as simple as the changing seasons. Maybe springtime reminds you of a time in your life when something tragic happened, and the sounds, smells and climate of that season rush you back toward that moment. Or maybe something horrible happened one New Year's Eve that you've never forgotten, and every year as December 31 rolls around, you are overcome with dread or fear. Where do all these negative emotions come from? Your mind.

Your mind is a breeding ground for Satan's attacks. He uses your thoughts to keep you chained to yesterday. He prevents you from experiencing God's best for your future by filling your mind with negativity and causing you to "remember when." You may be thinking, *But, Terri, I can't make the memories go away!* It's true, memories don't disappear, but you can stop them from consuming you. Being passive about it is not the solution.

When your memories are bigger than your dreams, you need to get aggressive. You need to take control over your mind—the battlefield—and start battling for the fight of your life. Really, have you ever thought about it? You are battling (and losing) for your life when you can't let go of the past.

It's time to get aggressive!

Put Up a Fight with the Right Enemy

Revelation 12:11 tells us, "They overcame him by the blood of the Lamb, and by the word of their testimony" (*KJV*). After suffering through many years of needless torment over my past, and after learning that the battle was in my mind, I can say that I am free from the painful reminders of my past. I figured out what works, and I want to share it with you. I've devoted this chapter to getting control over your thought life so that you can beat the devil at his game.

We give the devil too much access to our minds. Think about it. What *is* going on in your mind right now? What do you think about during the day? What do you think about when you lie down and close your eyes at night? What's the first thing on your mind when you wake up in the morning? Whatever you think about the most is the direction your life will go. If you think about your past long enough, you'll turn around and go right back to it.

I grew up in such a strong household of faith. My dad is known around the world as a pioneer in preaching the Word of Faith message. I grew up attending more church services in a month than most people would in an entire year. My parents took the time to teach me the Word of God and lived it by example before me. I read it. I studied it. I witnessed it. And I believed it.

At the same time, I found out that God is no respecter of persons, and neither is Satan. He could care less how many church services you've been to, whether or not your dad's a preacher, how long you pray, how many Christian books you have on your nightstand or how often you've read the Bible. He hates you, and he hates me, and he will use whatever he can to destroy our lives!

Do you know when Satan focuses his attacks on you? I've observed that it happens three times:

1. When you wake up
2. When you lay down at night
3. All day long

In other words, he never stops. It's a never-ending battle.

One of my most favorite quotes is, "You will never outgrow warfare; you must simply learn to fight." The key word in that statement is "you." *You* will never outgrow warfare; *you* have to learn to fight! The first part of fighting is realizing who the enemy is! It's not your parents; it's not your old boyfriend or old girlfriend; it's not your boss, your uncle, your neighbor, your pastor, your so-called friend or that person who violated you. It's Satan.

He's the one behind every attack, every temptation and every pain you've ever experienced. As Paul states, "For our struggle is not against flesh and blood, but against the rulers, against the authorities, against the powers of this dark world and against the spiritual forces of evil in the heavenly realms" (Eph. 6:12, *NIV*).

Have you ever watched a professional bullfight? The matador is dressed in a fancy costume and stands out in the middle of an open-air stadium packed full of bloodthirsty people eager to mock an angry bull. The matador holds the infamous red cloth in the air and dangles it in front of that bull. The bull rubs his foot in the dirt and charges after that cloth with everything in him. In a split second, the matador raises the cloth, the bull misses it and the crowd goes nuts . . . cheering, laughing and applauding the matador.

The bull circles around, this time salivating and grunting inside while the matador taunts him relentlessly by dangling the cloth as if to say, "Come and get it." The bull charges with all his power only to miss the red cloth and be laughed at again.

What's the problem? That bull is deceived. He thinks the red cloth is the enemy. If he only knew that the real enemy is the one *holding* the cloth, he could annihilate the matador in one charge. Yet for centuries the game has continued with the animal charging after the red cloth instead.

It's the same with you. Satan has been playing the same game for centuries on unsuspecting children of God. While Satan *is* our enemy, he makes us believe that other people and even God are the ones who are hurting us. We aim our frustrations at them;

meanwhile, Satan is laughing at and mocking us. Make no mistake. He's the one you need to charge toward with all your anger, pain and heartbreak. It's not the person who hurt you. Yes, that person was dangled in front of you, like a matador's cloth, but Satan is the one holding the cloth. He is the one behind every touch of destruction in your life.

As I've mentioned before, the Bible describes Satan as a thief (see John 10:10). When a thief breaks into a house, what does he steal? The paper cups, the napkins, the toaster? Of course not! He goes straight for what is valuable. The plasma screen TV, the jewelry, the computer, the cash. Well, *you* are what's valuable. You are the most precious thing to God. And that's exactly why Satan is attacking you so hard.

> When I gaze into star-studded skies and attempt to comprehend the vast distances, I contemplate in utter amazement my Creator's concern for me. I am dumbfounded that You should care personally about me. And yet You have made me in Your image. You have called me Your child and *chosen me* to be Your servant. You have assigned to me the fantastic responsibility of carrying on Your creative activity. O God, how full of wonder and splendor You are! (Ps. 8:3-5, *Psalms Now*).

If Satan can convince you to have a low self-esteem and be overwhelmed by guilt and shame, you will never have the confidence to go before God to obtain mercy and find grace to help you. Why? Because the shame will keep you at a distance from God. That's exactly what Satan's goal is—to keep you from God. When you avoid God, you will doubt His ability to hear your prayers and, even more, answer them.

It doesn't take a rocket scientist to figure out, as Beth Moore puts it, the "method to his [Satan's] madness." Satan is actively working hard to do everything he possibly can to keep you away from God. The more distant you are from God's plan for your life, the closer you are to his. The minute a child of God fully realizes she is a child of God, she begins to accept the rights and privileges that come with it. She begins to understand the power of fighting against the devil. She begins to understand the importance of speaking the Word in her life. And at that point, the devil walks away (for a while) with his tail between his legs.

But I Don't Want to Fight!

I've taken the popular personality test and found out that I fall under the category "phlegmatic/sanguine." In other words, I just wish we could all get along and have fun! Even where the devil is concerned, I've sometimes questioned, "Why does he have to be so mean?! Why can't we work something out?"

Well, once you discover that Satan hates you and has a calculated plan for your destruction, you realize that you better learn to fight or he will destroy you! Trust me; you don't want to work anything out with him! There is never a time when he has compassion for you or feels that he's put you through too much. No. The only things on his mind are to *kill, steal* and *destroy.*

I don't want to scare you off. I just want you to learn to fight. I want you to take this thing seriously and stop being mad at the wrong enemy. Stop blaming others for how your life has turned out. Stop blaming God, and stop condemning yourself for your mistakes. Get mad at the devil! Learn to fight him!

This realization has been such a challenge for me. One of my greatest weaknesses is that I have always been too dependent on people to take care of me, and I hate confrontation of any kind. I don't like fighting. I don't like competitions. I'm just not a real aggressive person.

I'm the younger of two sisters. My sister and I are polar opposites. She has always been the "take charge" type, and I've been the peacemaker who goes with the flow. She led and I followed. I allowed her to tend to my needs instead of being strong enough to take care of myself.

I fell into that same pattern with every guy I ever dated. I was drawn to leaders who enjoyed taking care of me. I found out later (through much studying of the Word) that I was even allowing *people* to fill the role of the Holy Spirit in my life. I wanted *them* to lead me, guide me, help me, comfort me and strengthen me. Since then I've learned to fight. I thank God every day that I'm not the same girl I used to be.

As I shared with you earlier, when my husband and I were nearly filing for divorce, this "peacemaker" was at a boiling point. We were attending marriage counseling (separately), and my therapist recognized immediately that I had a dependency on others to fight my battles. He was committed to teaching me how to be more independent. I remember him saying that if my husband and I ever worked things out, he wanted me to get back with him because I *wanted* to, not because I *needed* to.

During that season of my life, I was getting ready to go on a trip to New Orleans to visit a dear friend. Not accustomed to traveling alone, I was dreading it. The counselor said to me, "Pretend you're at the gate getting ready to board the plane. A nice gentleman says to you, 'Are you going to New Orleans?' and you answer, 'Yes.' He says, 'Can I carry your bag for you?' What are you going to say?"

I thought for a moment and said, "Ahhh . . . thank you so much. I would really appreciate that."

My counselor shook his head. "No. No. No, Terri. You're going to say, 'No, thank you. I don't need any help. I can carry them myself!'"

I pouted and responded, "But you don't know how heavy my bags are!"

My point? I've since had to grow up. I've had to become independent of people always telling me what I should do. I've had to admit my total dependency on God and God alone. I've had to get comfortable being alone with God and receiving my strength and direction from Him, and not others. I've had to learn to avoid all that distracts me from God's plan for my life by knowing my weaknesses and establishing boundaries in those weak areas. I've had to learn to crucify my desires, as painful as that process was, knowing that whatever God asks me to do is for my benefit, not for my harm. Finally, I've learned to fight!

Are You Ready?

Jesus said that Satan is "the father of lies" (John 8:44, *NIV*). If Satan is tormenting you, belittling you and accusing you, then you will automatically begin to accept his lies as the truth. As a result, you will live beneath what God has for you. You will settle for a life of insignificance, untapped potential and wasted years. Why? Because you believed a liar!

In 2 Corinthians 10:5, Paul says that in Jesus' name and authority, we are to be "casting down arguments and every high thing that exalts itself against the knowledge of God, bringing every thought into captivity to the obedience of Christ" (*NKJV*). I want you to get to a place in your life where you instantly get a hold of your thought life and make it line up with the Word of God. I want you to know how to defeat depression and negative thinking before it ever gets a hold on you. I want you to spend the rest of your life tormenting the devil for the torment he's put you through.

> Do not remember the former things, nor consider the things of old. Behold, I will do a new thing, now it shall spring forth; shall you not know it? (Isa. 43:18-19, *NKJV*).

This is an excellent Scripture for you to write down and even carry around with you. If you want to experience freedom from your past, I encourage you to memorize it and regularly confess it out of your mouth.

From this verse we understand that "remembering" and "considering" are both mental processes. They both take place in the mind. God is telling us to *not remember nor consider* the former things (the past). He wants to do a new thing in your life. A new thing! Can you believe that?

The Power of Your Mouth

The key to changing your life or going from . . .

- hopeless to hopeful
- discouraged to encouraged
- brokenhearted to being made whole
- depressed to joyful
- wounded to healed
- passive to aggressive
- existing to visionary

. . . all has to do with what is coming out of *your mouth*. Proverbs 18:21 says that what you say actually releases the power of life or death: "Death and life are in the power of the tongue, and those who love it will eat its fruit" (*NKJV*; see also Jas. 3:6; 1 Pet. 3:10). While the battle for your life is being fought in your mind, your mouth is the most powerful weapon you have against the enemy! It is *the* weapon in combatting your worst thoughts.

Let me explain. You defeat wrong thoughts with words, not with other thoughts. You can't try hard to think about something else until your bad thoughts go away. It's just a matter of time before your mind will go right back to where it wanted to be.

Imagine if I asked you to subtract 3,968 from 8,539. As you're subtracting in your head, what if I interrupted you and asked you to give me directions to your house. You would have to stop working the math problem in order to hear what your mouth was saying. Your words—giving me directions to your house—would take over the thoughts about the math problem. Try it.

I learned this years ago, but it took awhile to realize how powerful it is in mental warfare. Your mouth will cause you to go from constantly being under attack to being on the attack. When Satan comes at you with negative, oppressing thoughts, you will know how to shut him up. It's right under your nose. You just have to use it.

I heard a story years ago about a guy named Mike who played football for the Miami Dolphins. He was approached by the coach of Auburn University to help recruit new players for the team. The coach said to Mike, "You know, there's that kind of guy that you hit 'em and knock 'em down and they stay down."

Mike asked, "We don't want that kind of guy, do we, Coach?"

"Of course not," replied the coach. "But there's that other kind of guy that you hit 'em and knock 'em down and they get back up. No matter how many times you hit 'em and knock 'em down, they always get back up!"

Mike started getting excited and asked, "So we're going to go looking for that kind of player, right, Coach?"

"No, Mike. Find me the guy who's knocking everybody down!"

It's a great story and reminds me of what happens when you learn to pick up the Sword of the Spirit, which is the Word of God coming out of your mouth (see Eph. 6:17), and shut Satan's torment up! You become the one who is on the offense. You become the one charging after Satan rather than constantly fighting to stay on your feet on the defensive side. It's all in what you do with your mouth!

There are three things you must put in your mouth in order to get aggressive with the devil: thanks, praise and the Word of God.

Thanksgiving

In 1 Thessalonians 5:18, Paul says "Give thanks in all circumstances, for this is God's will for you in Christ Jesus" (*NIV*). If you want to experience the wholeness that God's Word talks about, then opening your mouth and giving thanks to God is key. It is the truth! It works. It's not a formula; it is based on a heart condition. If your heart is right, you will not be denied the healing power that comes from having a thankful heart.

I remember hearing a preacher tell me to "be thankful." My immediate response? "For what? That my entire life has fallen to pieces? That I've lost everything and don't even know what I'm supposed to do with my life? That I'm a confused mess? Sure, I'll be thankful! Yeah, right!" Sarcasm oozed out of me! But then this minister continued her message and said, "Begin thanking God for what's left in your life, and God will begin to move in your behalf."

Now that's powerful! Stop looking at what you've lost. Start looking at what you've got left! It's the nature of the flesh to look around at everything that's wrong and then complain about it. That is so easy to do. But I'm telling you, complaining will keep you stuck in your current situation year after year after year.

We saw this happen with the Israelites. They were coming out of bondage and headed for the Promised Land, but their mouths kept them bound. The Lord punished them for constantly complaining about how bad things were:

> How long will this wicked community grumble against me? . . . As surely as I live, declares the LORD, I will do to you the very things I heard you say: In this desert your bodies will fall—every one of you . . . who has grumbled against me. Not one of you will enter the land I swore with uplifted hand to make your home. . . . For forty years— one year for each of the forty days you explored the land— you will suffer for your sins and know what it is like to have me against you (Num. 14:27-30,34, *NIV*).

Because they complained, they remained in the wilderness for 40 years, circling the same ridiculous deserts and mountains when it should have taken only 11 days to get them through to the Promised Land! What a waste of time and energy!

It sounds so crazy to hear that story about the Israelites, doesn't it? If you're like me, you might be thinking, *Well, that was back then. That was actual wilderness and mountains. I can't relate to those people.* Well, what issue are you still dealing with that could have been dealt with in two weeks, but you are still harrassed by it, still hanging on to it and still talking about it? Has it been five years? Fifteen years? However long it's been, it's time to get free and move on. Complaining will only keep you off the path of healing and wholeness.

Think about your own life. Isn't it amazing how you can hear a bunch of compliments: *Your hair is beautiful. I like the way you're wearing your makeup. I love that dress. That color looks great on you.* And so on. But one negative comment like, *You look a little pale,* and all the compliments go out the window. All you think about the entire day is how pale you look. You don't remember that someone said your hair is beautiful, your makeup looks great, your dress is amazing. You just focus on the negative, looking pale. We ask other people, "Do I really look pale?" Then we try to make that person look bad by telling our friends, "Can you believe that woman told me I looked pale?"

We do that so many times with God. We magnify the negative things in our life and don't even notice or remember the positive things. God has done many things for you that you may have forgotten. Or maybe you just haven't given them any attention because Satan has diverted your attention to the bad stuff. As long as you're complaining, it's no different than opening the front door of your house and telling the devil to come right on in and take anything you've got! Don't do that! Slam the door in his face by giving thanks to God for what He has already done. And thank God for what He is about to do in your life. As Psalm 50:23 states, "He who sacrifices thank offerings honors me, and he prepares the way that I may show him the salvation of God" (*NIV*).

Giving thanks to God also causes His peace to rule in your heart: "And let the peace of God rule in your hearts, to which also you were called in one body; and be thankful" (Col. 3:15, *NKJV*). If you will begin to thank God for what you have instead of what you don't have, you will come out of your attack, slump, mess— whatever you want to call it—a lot sooner.

I remember when I finally surrendered to praising God instead of basking in my complaining. I had allowed Satan to magnify my problems so much that I really didn't think I had anything to be thankful for. And even if I did, I sure didn't want to talk about it. I wanted to talk about how bad things were. All I could see were the losses in my life.

It was a true turning point in my situation when I *made myself* lift my hands to heaven and literally cried out my thankfulness.

"Lord, I thank You for that little red-headed girl sleeping upstairs in her bed right now. Thank You for giving her to me."

"I thank You that I have a house, a beautiful house, to live in."

"I thank you for my health."

"I thank you that I have a good job."

"I thank you that I have a car to drive."

"I thank you that I have food."

"I thank you for my best friend."

When you look around at what is left instead of all that is lost, you will see that you actually do have many things to be thankful for. When you are giving thanks, your mind is thinking about something other than your problems. You have your mind off of the problem and on the solution: God. You are also giving God an open door to work miracles in your life. When you begin to give thanks, you have the ear of God directed toward your heart.

Do you want to be healed of all the pain in your life? Do you want a special touch from God? Do you want to get to a place in your life where the hurt is gone? Do you want to be made whole? Being thankful is the key to all these things. Let's look at a story in the Bible that illustrates this point. It's found in Luke 17:11-19.

Ten lepers approached Jesus. They asked for healing, and He made them whole. They left at Jesus' command to show the priests that they had been healed, but one leper who was a Samaritan turned around and thanked Jesus first. He was incredibly grateful that he had been healed.

Jesus appreciated this man's gratitude and asked, "Didn't I heal ten men? Where are the other nine? Has no one returned to give glory to God except this foreigner?" (v. 17, *NLT*). Then Jesus said to the man, "Stand up and go. Your faith has healed you" (v. 19, *NLT*). *The Amplified Bible* says, "Your faith (your trust and confidence that spring from your belief in God) has restored you to health." The *King James Version* states, "Thy faith hath made thee whole."

There were 10 lepers; nine of them were healed and went on their way. Only one turned back to simply say, "Thank you." And the one who gave thanks was not only healed but completely made whole from the inside out.

I love the way that my dad explains this story. He explains that leprosy is a flesh-eating disease. When people had leprosy, their body parts, maybe an ear or an arm, were usually decaying or completely missing. Leprosy was a very visible disease. When Jesus healed the lepers, the nine who walked away experienced no more leprosy. In other words, the disease stopped eating away at their flesh from that point on. However, whatever leprosy they had experienced up to that time was still recognizable. They still had missing limbs.

The one who gave thanks, however, was completely made whole. This meant there were no signs that he had ever had leprosy! Wow! Isn't that encouraging? You can get to a place of healing in your life where you have no signs of past sexual abuse; no signs of depression; no signs of abortion; no signs of addiction; no signs of having been tormented!

That's how much God values a thankful heart. Some people are thankful but they never say so, so it blesses no one. Express your gratitude and appreciation with your mouth. Psalm 100:4 says, "Enter into His gates with thanksgiving and a thank offering and into His courts with praise! *Be thankful and say so* to Him, bless and affectionately praise His name!" (*AMP*, emphasis added).

Here's another thought: When you give thanks, don't just thank God for what you already have; thank Him for what you are believing you will receive. Thanking God ahead of time is the highest expression of your faith and trust in God.

It's no different than if I told my daughter, "I'm going to buy you a new outfit." She would instantly respond, "Thank you, Mommy," before she even saw the outfit. Why? Because she believes my word. She knows I'll do what I said I would do. She trusts me. She doesn't say, "I'll believe it when I see it. I'll just save my thanks until I get the dress, thank you very much." If she did, I would probably think of her as a spoiled little brat who doesn't really deserve a new outfit.

We aren't any different when we wait until God does something for us before we thank Him. We need to thank Him because He already promised in His Word what He will do. Show Him that you trust Him by giving thanks ahead of time. Thank Him for how His healing power will turn even the bad things that have happened to you into places of strength and authority in His calling on your life (see Rom. 8:28). Thank Him for healing your life, delivering you from bondage and restoring your marriage, your finances, your dreams and your broken heart. It's a powerful way to slam the door shut on the devil's evil schemes and open the door to God's power and blessings.

Praise

Praise is another weapon in your arsenal whereby you can defeat the enemy. You have been given this weapon, but you have to pick it up and use it. Is it easy? NO. But it does work. I am so passionate and convinced of this truth because it has saved my life. I wrote a little about this in the second chapter and want to continue on the subject here.

The best part about using praise in order to combat negative memories in your mind is that praise causes Satan to shut up. It silences him. He cannot come at you when you open your mouth and begin praising God! Psalm 8:2 tells us, "Out of the mouths of babes and unweaned infants, You have established strength because of Your foes, that you might *silence* the *enemy* and the *avenger*" (*AMP*, emphasis added). Jesus quoted this passage from the psalms when He was confronted by the religious leaders of His day:

> But when the chief priests and the scribes saw the wonderful things that He did and the boys and the girls and the youths and the maidens crying out in the porches and courts of the temple, Hosanna (O be propitious, graciously inclined) to the Son of David! they were indignant. And they said to Him, Do You hear what these are saying? And Jesus replied to them, Yes; have you never read, Out of the mouths of babes and unweaned infants *You have made (provided) perfect praise?* (Matt. 21:15-16, *AMP*).

What should Psalm 8:2 mean to you? Let's look at this verse. It says that out of praise, He has established strength so that you might silence the enemy and the avenger! "Silence" means to restrain, or cause to sit down. "Enemy" means a hostile adversary who literally hates you. "Avenger" means one looking for revenge.

According to Psalm 8:2 and Matthew 21:15-16, we see that praise strengthens you and causes the enemy (Satan) to be restrained or silenced! That is encouraging, especially if Satan has been screaming in your ear for some time now, telling you how things will never change. All you have to do is open your mouth and give praise to Jesus, and it causes Satan to be silenced!

One day I was out taking my little 10-pound Pomeranian dog, Ashton, for a walk in the park. As we got closer to the park, I noticed a Rotweiler across the field. Ashton and this mean-looking dog spotted each other. Suddenly, the Rotweiler, who was glaring ferociously at my Ashton, with saliva drooling from his mouth, came charging after us. I thought, "Oh, Jesus, help us! I don't want to see a little hot dog get eaten!"

The angry dog took off with harmful intentions; but in a moment, the dog was jerked back. He fell over on his side, sat up on his back legs and helplessly looked at us. His owner had one of those constraining leashes that he pulled back on so the dog couldn't travel far. I stared at the dog and felt his eyes saying, "I'd come at you if I could, but I can't, because I'm restrained!"

This is what happens in the spirit realm when you open your mouth and begin praising God. It puts Satan on a leash. It causes him to sit down and shut up. He looks at you, growling but helpless, and says, "I'd come at you if I could, but I can't, because I'm restrained!"

Satan doesn't want peace in your mind. He doesn't want you to think you have any reason to praise God. He doesn't want change in your life. He doesn't even want you to finish this book. And he certainly doesn't want you to know how powerful praise is, because that is when he becomes powerless against you. Praise is your weapon.

There have been numerous instances when I have defeated the enemy by leaving a room and going somewhere by myself to praise God. When you realize how intimidating praise is to the devil, it makes you want to glorify God that much more! If there's anything Satan hates, it is hearing a believer praise the One he hates the most—Jesus!

Praise confuses Satan. He gets so flustered when he's launched an all-out attack against you; when he's fired his best shot, hoping to wipe you out, and suddenly he sees you walking around your house with your hands lifted up, shouting, "I praise You, Jesus, You are my Deliverer! Thank You for delivering me. Praise You, Jesus, that You are my Prince of Peace, and You are restoring peace to my mind and my heart. Praise You, Jesus, You are faithful and powerful. I praise Your name because it is above all other names!" The devil doesn't know what to think.

I love the story of Jehoshaphat, a leader of the nation of Israel, told in 2 Chronicles 20. Jehoshaphat was alerted by some messengers that a massive army was on its way to destroy the nation. Jehoshaphat was stunned and didn't know what to do. He even admitted to God that even if he did know what to do, he didn't have the strength to do it.

Still, he kept his eyes on God. Jehoshaphat sought God for direction, strength and wisdom. While in the middle of going to battle, he didn't send the best fighters to the frontline; he sent the "praisers" of the army, almost like today's marching band and chorus. This tactic so bewildered the opposing army that the enemy began to kill each other, not the Israelites.

When he had consulted with the people, he appointed singers to sing to the Lord and praise Him in their holy [priestly] garments as they went out before the army, saying, "Give thanks to the Lord, for His mercy and loving-kindness endure forever!" (2 Chron. 20:21, *AMP*).

When you feel you have no reason to praise God, that's when you need to do it the most. When you've lost a lot of money, when your heart is broken, when your marriage is falling apart, when you're lonely, in that midnight hour of crying—that's when you need to lift your hands to heaven and begin praising God for who He is and what He has promised to do in your life.

You can praise God by simply saying, "Lord, I praise You that You said You would never leave me nor forsake me. You're right here with me. You said that I have nothing to fear. Thank You, Lord, for being with me right now. Thank You that You perfect that which concerns me. Thank You for comforting me. Thank You for healing my broken heart."

Praise will cause the heaviness to lift off of you. I felt it happen in my own life. Many times I have praised God and felt a physical burden released from my body. Sometimes it would lift for only five minutes and I'd have to do it again and again. I would go to sleep praising God under my breath in order to make the thoughts shut up. I even made myself get into a habit of waking up and putting praise in my mouth as the first thing that comes out.

I caught on to the fact that Satan was waiting for me to wake up so he could begin the torment. It backfired on him. Now as soon as my alarm goes off, I open my eyes and immediately say,

"I praise You, Jesus. You are amazing!" I know Satan hates seeing me wake up in the morning!

When you praise, oppression will lift. Your circumstances will change. The torment will cease. Need a little more proof of the power in praise? Remember the story of Paul and Silas in the prison cell (see Acts 16:25-26)? They had been sitting in prison chained up and bound. They did not deserve what was happening to them. They had been unjustly tried, found guilty when they were innocent and beaten mercilessly. They could have easily cried, complained and blamed God. What did they do to get free? They praised.

> But about midnight, as Paul and Silas were praying and singing hymns of praise to God, and the [other] prisoners were listening to them, suddenly there was a great earthquake, so that the very foundations of the prison were shaken; and at once all the doors were opened and everyone's shackles were unfastened (Acts 16:25-26, *AMP*).

When they opened their mouths, with pain piercing through their bodies, Paul and Silas praised God. Everyone heard them, including the other prisoners and the guards. As they were shouting out to God, an earthquake shook the ground, the walls of the prison began to shake and the chains binding their ankles and wrists fell off. Paul and Silas were free!

Amen! If you want to be free from the chains that Satan has put around you, then lift your hands to God and praise Him. Praise Him loudly. Don't be ashamed, embarrassed or insecure. Be determined to be set free! Yell, jump, run and shout your praises to God. Be willing to make a fool of yourself. I have, plenty of times. If anyone was watching during my praise sessions, they would have seen me running around my house declaring, "I'm free. I'm free. I'm free. I'm not the girl I used to be!" But when you're desperate and so grateful for freedom, you couldn't care less about looking foolish! All you want to do is to praise God.

Praise is the shortest distance between you and God. Praise will set you free. Praise will cause the bondages in your life to break off of you!

The Word of God

All we have to do is look at the story of Jesus in the wilderness being tempted by the devil to see how powerful the Word of God is. Every time Satan tried to get Jesus to sin or fall into temptation, Jesus used this life-changing tool to defeat the devil. It sent him packing every time.

Your mouth has the power to choose the direction of your life. Proverbs 18:21 says, "Death and life are in the power of the tongue" (*AMP*). How did God create the world? With the words of His mouth. Throughout Genesis, we read a number of statements that begin with "God said . . . and it was so." In other words, when God wants something to happen, to change or to be created, He speaks! He doesn't just think it or wish it; He declares it out of His mouth!

Whining and complaining will not change anything. Speaking God's Word, however, will begin to shape your thoughts and your future. The Word of God contains a power that has the ability to change everything. Now, I'm not talking about reciting a particular verse over and over like a robot or using some context of Scripture to "name it and claim it." I'm talking about believing that God wrote His Word for you and declaring His promises over your life.

"As it is written: 'I have made you a father of many nations.' He is our father in the sight of God, in whom he believed—the God who gives life to the dead and calls things that are not as though they were" (Rom. 4:17, *NIV*). God calls things that don't exist as if they do exist. He expects you to do the same thing. We see this in the story of Elijah told in 1 Kings 18. Elijah knew that the Lord had said He would send rain on the land (see 1 Kings 18:1). After three years of drought had passed, Elijah declared to King Ahab that the Lord's word had been completed—before the rain ever reached the land of Israel! Elijah declared, "Go, eat and drink, for there is the sound of a heavy rain" (v. 41, *NIV*).

Jesus taught us to speak forth God's Word the way that Elijah did: "Have faith in God. For assuredly, I say to you, whoever says to this mountain, 'Be removed and be cast into the sea,' and does not doubt in his heart, but believes that those things he says will be done, he will have whatever he says" (Mark 11:22). We have to speak what we believe as if it's already happening in our life. That's called releasing our faith!

"I am God, and there is none like Me, *declaring the end* and the result from the beginning" (Isa. 46:9-10, *AMP*, emphasis added). God wants you to do what He does. Declare the end result of what you believe for in your life before you ever see any sign of it happening. I know it sounds crazy, and you will feel ridiculous the first time or two you do this, but it contains power like no other weapon you have.

When you look at the story of David and Goliath, you will notice that David actually killed Goliath with his words before he ever released the stone! The Bible tells us that Goliath *said* to David. The devil speaks to us in the same way Goliath spoke to David. So what is our defense? Speaking back to him!

> Then said David to the Philistine, You come to me with a sword, a spear, and a javelin, but I come to you in the name of the Lord of hosts, the God of the ranks of Israel, Whom you have defied. This day the Lord will deliver you into my hand, and I will smite you and cut off your head. And I will give the corpses of the army of the Philistines this day to the birds of the air and the wild beasts of the earth, that all the earth may know that there is a God in Israel (1 Sam. 17:45-46, *AMP*).

David spoke to his giant, the enemy, before he ever released the stone. He killed Goliath with his words first! He prophesied his enemy's death with the words of his mouth! You cannot defeat your "giant" with your mouth shut. Whatever giant is in your life—your emotions, your weight, your money, your marriage, loneliness, anxiety, stress, depression—whatever it is that tries to intimidate you, speak to it and use the Word of God!

You might be thinking, *Where do I start? The Bible is such a big book. I feel overwhelmed!* That's exactly what I used to think. I used to hear messages like this and get stirred up inside because I knew it was the Truth, but I didn't know which Scriptures to confess. Or I would have good intentions to do the research of finding Scriptures that applied to what I was going through, but never really got around to doing it. I'm going to help you out.

In the "chapter challenge" section at the end of this book, you'll find some of my favorite verses in the Bible that you can use today to speak good things over your life. This is not a hard thing to do. All you have to do is make a decision to do it. Realize the power God's Word contains to heal your heart, calm your mind and revolutionize your life!

You can put a bookmark in this section of the book and set aside five minutes a day to open it up and speak these portions of Scripture out of your mouth. You may even want to write a few of them down and put them on your bathroom mirror, your refrigerator, your coffee pot or the dashboard of your car. Pretty soon, these words will get down in your spirit and you'll know them by heart. When the devil attacks your mind—which he will, probably before you even finish this chapter (if he has not done so already)—the Word of God will come up out of you! Now that is prophesying his defeat in your life!

One last thing: The biggest lesson I've learned in getting healed from all the hurts in my life is that it takes discipline. It takes doing the same things over and over every day. This is not just a one-time deal. It's a continuous process. The key to change is consistency. Satan doesn't take a day off, and neither can you.

"Do not merely listen to the word, and so deceive yourselves. Do what it says" (Jas. 1:22, *NIV*). I promise you: the more you do what the Word says, the more the devil will leave you alone. You must confess Scripture over your life until whatever you are confessing comes to pass. Old Testament scholars note that when God changed Abram's name in Genesis 17:5, He changed it from Abram, meaning "exalted father," to Abraham, meaning "father of multitude." For the entire year before Isaac, the son whom God had promised, was born, Abraham was proclaiming through the very meaning of his new name God's promise to him that he would have a multitude of decendants.

Don't give up on God or His Word. It is the Truth. It is the highest form of reality that exists. His Word never fails. If anything fails, it's our ability to stick with it. Just because your deliverance doesn't happen overnight, don't give up. Get aggressive and become bolder.

Every single time you thank the Lord when you don't feel like it, things are changing in the spirit realm. Every time you get up in the middle of the night and just start praising Jesus for who He is in your life, things are changing in the spirit realm. Every time you confess a Scripture from the Word of God when you'd rather call up your friend and cry and complain, things are changing in the spirit realm. You may not see the changes yet, but you will. Of this, I am sure.

6

WHEN YOU'RE TEMPTED TO GO BACK... *YOU COULD BE FALLING INTO A TRAP*

In chapter 1, you saw in the story of Lot's wife that any temptation to look back will destroy your life. So why would you even think about it? Because something back there still grabs your attention! And Satan, the deceiver, knows it. He knows where you are weak and he knows where you are strong. He will repeatedly bring the very temptation that appeals to your greatest vulnerabilities, hoping to break you down and cause you to give in. Your job is to wise up to his tactics and stay focused on what's ahead.

The Lures of Deception

Satan's game is deception. He can only defeat you by first deceiving you. Where? In your mind. Being deceived is nothing more than unknowingly believing a lie. That explains why Satan has to be so subtle and crafty.

As much as I loathe mice, I'll use their behavior as an example to show you how Satan works. Would a mouse step on a trap to get the cheese if it had full knowledge that it will kill him? Would it satisfy a temporary desire only to die in the process? Most likely not. So the trap, therefore, has to be deceiving. The cheese has to be the focal point, not the trap. Satan works the same way with you. He must deceive you in order for you to fall for his well-disguised trap. If you've found yourself in a sinful situation, you can count on the fact that you've been deceived.

The only way you can uncover deception is by hearing the truth (which is what you are doing right now by reading this book). Psalm 119:130 says that the entrance of God's Word gives light. When I'm traveling for the ministry, there are times when I stay in a different hotel room each night of the week. I've awakened to go to the bathroom in the middle of the night when it was pitch-black. Not remembering where I am, I have crashed into walls, stepped on my shoes on the floor and walked into chairs in my disorientation. Because it's so dark, I can't see a thing. But as soon as I flip on the light, I see things I couldn't see in the dark. And I now know what to avoid so I don't get hurt *next time*.

God's Word is a light. When you begin hearing, reading and studying God's Word on a regular basis, it's like flipping on the light switch. God's Word (the "Light") begins to overcome all the darkness, and it prevents you from falling for the devil's same tricks the next time.

Satan is disguised, wearing a mask that is purposed to lure you. He knows what you will fall for and what you won't fall for. He's very observant of your weaknesses and knows what will get you thinking about things you shouldn't be thinking about.

You may be asking, *How does the devil know my weaknesses?* Because he has tested you, he has watched you, and he has made detailed notes of where you are vulnerable and where you suffer the greatest weaknesses in your life. If he is going to distract you and get you to lose your focus, he knows he must use something that specifically appeals to you. What appeals to you may not appeal to me. What makes me weak may not make you weak. What gets me distracted may not get you distracted. Satan will use whatever he can to grab your attention based on what he knows about you.

Here are some things he may tempt you with:

- Something you feel is missing in your life
- Something that makes you feel better
- Something that feeds your desires and needs
- Something that fills a void
- Something that heals the loneliness you feel inside
- Something from your past that you used to enjoy
- Something that feeds your ego
- Something that makes you feel pretty and wanted

Whatever lure Satan uses on you isn't coincidental. It is carefully thought out and planned. He wants to do whatever he can to make you lose your focus. He wants you to give in to whatever appeals to your flesh, because he knows it ultimately leads to death. "We are tempted when we are drawn away and *trapped* by our own evil desires. Then our evil desires conceive and give birth to sin; and sin, when it is full-grown, gives birth to death. Do not be deceived, my dear friends!" (Jas. 1:14-16, *TEV*, emphasis added).

What Lures You?

I'm not the "fishing type," but my husband is. I like to call him "Fishing Rod." I've noticed that he uses different lures whenever he goes fishing. I think it's interesting that the term for what you use to catch a fish is "lures." It does exactly what it says; it *lures* the fish to the bait. A fisherman knows which lure to use to attract either a catfish or a bass. He doesn't use the same lure for every fish. He uses the one that is custom-designed for *that* fish!

So how does he know which lure to use? He tests it. He dangles that bait in front of the fish, teasing it to see if the fish will fall for it. The fisherman may discover after a full day of fishing that the fish just isn't falling for it! So he goes back another day. He dangles another bait over and over to see if it's a temptation for the creature. Once he sees the fish fall for it, he makes a mental note: *Use this particular bait for this fish—works every time!*

Now, the fish isn't necessarily stupid. It doesn't understand that the lure is a trap in disguise. The hook isn't visible; only the lure can be seen. If the fish could see the hook, it would never try to get the lure. It wouldn't fall for the trap.

It's no different with Satan. His schemes and tactics are to attract you to a deceiving lure that will hook you and kill you. He sees you glancing in the direction of his bait. He sees you licking your lips and wondering what this bait would taste like. He continues to dangle it in front of you over and over and over until finally your curiosity gets the best of you, the temptation is too strong to resist, you've lost your focus and you fall for the bait.

Then, the very thing that lured you, the thing that once captured your heart, leads to your death: "For if you live according to the flesh you will die; but if by the Spirit you put to death the deeds of the body, you will live" (Rom. 8:13, *NKJV*). Death will be manifest all around you. It could be the death of your family, your vision, your marriage, your finances, your career, your confidence, your peace.

What traps have you discovered laid out for you? What is it that tempts you? What causes you to turn your head away from

God's plan? What has a hold over you? What is it that you still desire and know is wrong but you can't seem to shake it? What does Satan dangle in front of you every now and then, hoping you'll begin to desire it again? Is it drugs? Alcohol? Anger? Lust? The past? Unforgiveness? A person? A relationship?

Whatever it is, it's a trap created to kill you!

You may need to read this chapter over and over again. I have books with paragraphs similar to the ones I'm writing right now that I have highlighted. I read them over and over because they opened my eyes to the truth. They made me realize that what I'm going through and the feelings I'm having are not coincidental. They are part of the warfare I am in. They are designed to get me craving that particular thing that appeals to my flesh rather than going after what God wants me to do. I have to be reminded of these things daily. As I've said before, Satan never sleeps, and neither can we. We always need to stay on guard: "Stay alert. The Devil is poised to pounce, and would like nothing better than to catch you napping" (1 Pet. 5:8, *THE MESSAGE*).

Truths to Help You Wake Up and Fight

In order to recognize and not fall for the traps Satan has meticulously laid out for you, there are three things you must keep in mind.

God Has a Custom-Designed Assignment for Your Life

What God has designed for you is specially prepared to fit your individual strengths, talents, gifts, pleasures, hobbies and personality. He wants you to fulfill your assignment within your allotted time on earth. In other words, you have a "clipboard" with your name on it (refer back to the beginning of the first chapter). You do not have all the time in the world to get it done. That's why God needs you focused on fulfilling His plan for your life. He does not want you wasting the time He has given you on all the distractions of Satan. How disappointing would that be! "Before I [God] made you in your mother's womb, I chose you. Before you were born, I set you apart for a special work" (Jer. 1:5, *NCV*).

Satan Also Has a Custom-Designed Assignment for Your Life

Satan's design for your life is specially prepared to appeal to your greatest vulnerabilities. His plan is to ultimately distract you from God's plan. "Don't be so naïve and self-confident. You're not exempt. You could fall flat on your face as easily as anyone else. Forget about self-confidence; it's useless. Cultivate God-confidence" (1 Cor. 10:12, *THE MESSAGE*).

You Need a Custom-Designed Plan to Stay Focused on God's Assignment

I am such a firm believer in the phrase "Failing to plan is planning to fail." I believe that you need to have a custom-designed plan to keep you focused on God's assignment for your life or you will be more tempted to fall for Satan's. Remember, Satan's plan appeals to your flesh. God's plan appeals to your spirit, your conscience—the real you inside. You need to remember that "God is faithful. He will not allow the temptation to be more than you can stand. When you are tempted, he will show you a way out so that you can endure" (1 Cor. 10:13, *NLT*).

How to Avoid Getting Lured into Sin

So what do you have to know to find your way out of temptation? Here are five key ways to avoid Satan's lures.

1. Know What Tempts You

You need to know the areas of your vulnerability. For the most part, I believe you know where you are tempted. You know where that weak spot is that you try to make strong but often give in to. You know it's not right, but you can't seem to resist. So what is that area for you? What is that weak spot where it feels like Satan has you pinned? Is it lust? Is it premarital sex? Is it getting high with your friends? Is it watching pornography or searching sex Internet sites? Is it lying when it's not even necessary, but you just can't seem to quit? Is it alcohol that you secretly drink without the rest of your family knowing?

Why do you keep giving in to the temptation, over and over? Because it hurts too bad to stop. It hurts too bad to imagine getting away from the situation or telling yourself you can't have it anymore. You may have allowed Satan to convince you that the pain will be too much for you to endure. He is a liar. He is a deceiver. He is a manipulator. Don't fall for his bait!

I heard T. D. Jakes once give an illustration along these lines. He says that at best, you will experience 80 percent of life. Satan will dangle the other 20 percent in front of you. He'll say, "You don't have this 20 percent. You're missing this 20 percent. Wouldn't life be so much better if you had this 20 percent? How can you go on in life without this 20 percent? You're missing out!" Finally, Satan convinces you that you absolutely cannot go on in life without that 20 percent, so you give up the 80 percent you had for the 20 percent you didn't have, and now you're left with only 20 percent—exactly what Satan wanted!

If Satan can get you looking in the wrong direction (at that 20 percent) and looking at it too long, your whole life will turn in that direction. Mike Murdock puts it this way: "The only reason men fail is broken focus."[1] We must heed Paul's warning to "be well balanced (temperate, sober of mind), be vigilant and cautious at all times; for that enemy of yours, the devil, roams around like a lion roaring (in fierce hunger), seeking someone to seize upon and devour" (1 Pet. 5:8, *AMP*).

Satan will try to make you believe these weaknesses are not that big of a deal. He hopes you will ignore them because you think there is no need to worry about it, and it's even kinda fun. This is a lie you cannot believe. One temptation leads to another to another to another, and the next thing you know, you're trapped! You're suffocating under the mess you've allowed in your life.

"The little foxes . . . spoil the vines" (Song of Sol. 2:15, *NKJV*). It's the little compromises we make that can end up destroying our lives. The phone call we should have ignored. The dinner date we should have refused. The email we shouldn't have answered. The drink we should have resisted. The text message we shouldn't have sent. The door we shouldn't have opened.

Satan can't read your mind or perceive your thoughts, but he watches you. He listens to what you say. He watches what you do, and when he observes a weakness in your flesh, he says, "Ah-hah!

That's where I can get her!" And then he creates a plan. Is it co-incidental that most of your mistakes in the past have all been pretty much the same? Not at all. Perhaps you have been in one abusive relationship after another. Is that a coincidence? No! Maybe you got delivered from one addiction and now you find yourself addicted to a different substance. Coincidence? No.

If you choose to do what you know inside God is telling you to do—to walk away from that particular temptation—you will walk into a level of peace that you have only dreamed about in the past. You will be happy. You will be fulfilled. You will be free. "Happy is the man who doesn't give in and do wrong when he is tempted, for afterwards he will get as his reward the crown of life that God has promised to those who love him" (Jas. 1:12, *TLB*).

2. Know that You Need to Be Obedient

In Ephesians 5:10, Paul says, "Figure out what will please Christ, and then do it" (*THE MESSAGE*). God is telling you something. You may not hear His voice audibly, but He is constantly talking to you and revealing His instructions for you (see Job 33:14).

He may talk to you through a paragraph in a magazine article. You may be walking into your bedroom where the television is on, when someone says something that grabs your attention and speaks right to your situation. God speaks to you through your pastor at church, through your friends and through His Word. The hard part is obeying His Word!

Your obedience to whatever God is telling you to do is simply a reflection of your love for Him. "If you love me, you will obey my commandments" (John 14:15, *TEV*). That verse can be comforting or it can be convicting! If you truly love God and want to be in His perfect will for your life, then it will require your total obedience. Every step of obedience proves your love for God more than your love for others or things or having your own way. And God always rewards obedience.

I'm only sharing with you what God so gently *hammered* repeatedly in my life. If you don't fully obey what you know, deep in your heart, God is telling you to do, you will never move beyond your current circumstances. You will struggle with the same mess year after year.

How do you know if you are disobeying God? One sure sign of disobedience is a lack of peace, or confusion. That should be your number-one indicator that you are not following God's ultimate plan for your life. If you feel anxiety or confusion, then Satan has way too much control over your thoughts and over your decisions.

I don't believe we set out to disobey God. I believe that we know the difference between right and wrong, but we convince ourselves to continue doing wrong for many reasons:

We doubt our ability to hear from God.

We feel like doing it.

It's hard to obey.

It hurts too bad to stop doing the wrong thing.

It's uncomfortable to obey.

It's not what our flesh "wants" to do.

We don't think we can endure the pain we will feel inside.

We are just waiting for God to change us.

We don't want another person to be mad or angry at us.

This is not a comprehensive list. No matter what the cause is, the result is the same. Disobedience leaves the door wide open for Satan to come in and ruin your life. Disobedience brings with it every curse. This is no joke; it's serious.

On the other hand, obedience is the open door for God to bring every good thing into your life: peace, joy, hope, healing, wealth, restoration, and so on. Every act of obedience brings a blessing with it. This is great news. And it's something you better stay focused on in order to get through the pain that comes from obeying God.

> Blessed are those who endure when they are tested. When they pass the test, they will receive the crown of life that God has promised to those who love Him (Jas. 1:12, *GOD'S WORD*).

What does it mean for *you* to obey God? It may mean that you need to move. You may need to pack your things and get out of where you are living right now. You've known it for a long time now, but you have justified why you should stay. Don't reason with God. Reasoning with God only justifies sin and keeps you bound.

Obeying God may mean that you need to stay somewhere you'd like to leave. You may be trying to run from a situation or a relationship that God wants you in. Trust me, He knows something you don't know. He knows the end from the beginning. If God is telling you to stay, it's for your benefit. He would never want you to stay somewhere and remain miserable. If He's telling you to stay, it's because He plans to bring such healing and restoration to that situation that one day you will look back and say, "Thank God, I didn't leave."

I speak from much pain and experience when I write this. I know how hard it is to obey God. I also know what it's like to struggle internally for years, wondering why I was still hurting. See, I thought I was obeying God, only to find out later that I was only partially obeying. Because of that, I stayed miserable. I justified it by saying it was better than outright total disobedience. The truth is, partial obedience is still disobedience.

I can remember one particular time in my life when I was struggling so hard to get out of a relationship that I knew God had instructed me to get out of. I get sick to my stomach thinking of the number of times I came home crying because of the pain I was feeling inside. My flesh was fighting with everything in me to not obey God. I felt so alone and so weak.

The phone would ring, and I knew it was the guy I was not supposed to be in relationship with. So I just let it ring. It hurt so bad. All I wanted was to talk to him, to go out with him, to feel safe in his arms. What was so wrong with just one more date, one more phone call or one more letter? Everything was wrong with it. Partial obedience is still disobedience, and disobedience keeps us in bondage. Peace comes from obeying God. Torment comes from disobeying God.

I believe that as you are reading this, God is revealing things specifically to you. I believe that you are being honest with yourself about the areas of your life where you have partially obeyed God, and now you realize why things still haven't changed; why you're still struggling; why you're still confused; why you're still hurting inside; why you still feel like something is dragging behind you, weighing you down. You haven't made a clean break from your past. "With promises like this to pull us on, dear friends, let's make a clean break with everything that defiles or distracts us, both within and without" (2 Cor. 7:1, *THE MESSAGE*).

God will not advance your instructions beyond your last act of disobedience. If you're crying out for freedom from your past, and you want God to show you His will for your life, I have the answer. Go back to the last thing He told you to do and check to see if you did it. If you didn't, He will keep taking you back to it until you finally decide that God's way is the only way to true life. I would not be writing this book if I had not endured the pain from finally making myself obey!

3. Know that Obeying God Is Not Easy

Whatever God wants you to do, you need to know up front that it will not be easy. It wasn't easy for me, but the joy I experienced from all the heartache far outweighed the pain.

Obeying God will hurt initially. Satan will try to scare you into thinking that you will not be able to bear the pain that your soul (your mind, your will and your emotions) is feeling. He will play with your mind, bombard your emotions and try his best to convince you that you will forever be miserable if you obey God. You know what? The devil is lying to you. Read this verse as a warning:

> Watch out! Don't let evil thoughts or doubts make any of you turn from the living God (Heb. 3:12, *CEV*).

Jesus said, "If anyone would come after me, he must deny himself and take up his cross and follow me" (Mark 8:34, *NIV*). When you deny yourself and do not give in to the temptation to go back to your old ways, old addictions, old relationships or whatever it is you're longing for, you will experience a type of suffering in your flesh. Even Jesus did. When Jesus was alone in the Garden of Gethsemane, just before going to the cross, He knew that He had to obey God. Did He want to? Was He incredibly excited to carry out the plan of salvation? Of course not. Jesus didn't want to go through the agony and pain to fulfill His assignment, but He knew He needed to do so. He had to look beyond the pain at what He would gain. Thank God He did. Because of His painful obedience in dying on the cross, it saved our lives. And yes, it did hurt Him.

Someone in need is waiting on the other side of your obedience right now. Did you read that? There are people who need you to share with them what you have been through to help them get out of the mess they are in. You have a story. You have a testimony. You have the wounds to prove that you've been through tough times. Note the grammatical tense "been through." In other words, you came out on the other side! Even today, someone in need is waiting on the other side of your obedience.

When you obey God, your flesh will be crucified. There is a suffering that comes from denying our flesh what it desires or wants to do. The Bible reveals to us that Jesus suffered so severely (in obedience to God) that He sweat drops of blood. Can you picture that? He was in the garden alone, probably feeling like the loneliest man in the world. He was in incredible mental anguish over what He was required to do in order to fulfill God's assignment for His life. Jesus struggled just like we all struggle. He was sovereign Lord clothed in human flesh. If Jesus suffered . . . if it was hard for Him, what makes us any different?

When you are committed to obeying God, you have to trust Him more than ever. When what God is telling you to do is in complete opposition to what your flesh wants to do, you have got the biggest war on your hands. That's why reading books like this one is imperative in order to keep your eyes focused on the truth about what you're going through, not just the fact that it is difficult.

You can't continue listening to all those voices in your head that are trying to keep you in bondage. You have to be reminded of God's Word. You have to be reminded that deliverance is on its way. You have to be reminded that the pain won't last forever. You have to be reminded that feelings are only temporary.

Let me warn you one more time: When you decide to obey God in whatever He's telling you to do, your feelings will not support you. In fact, they will be screaming against you. Your emotions will lie to you, telling you that you can't endure this. You'll feel like you're not going to make it. It's too hard. It's too painful. It's too much work. I'm telling you that you must trust God and His Word more than your feelings, and cling to your heavenly Father for life! That's exactly what God wants you to do. The good news is that He will never let you go.

4. Know that Each Day Counts

In chapter 4, I shared with you the necessity of having a daily plan to keep you focused. It is essential that you do this. You must get your mind on a daily plan that leads to the fulfillment of your dreams, or your head will automatically go back to what is familiar . . . especially old distractions. Remember, fulfilling your destiny, or God's plan for your life, isn't the result of one big event. It's a result of daily habits and choices.

Live each day on purpose. Don't waste time. Time is the most precious thing that you have. Review your daily goals and make an intentional decision to stay focused. If you slip up, don't quit. Start over.

Just last week, I left a meeting at the office and was feeling confused. I know that God is not the author of confusion, but I was flat-out confused. I got in my car during lunchtime and went to get my daily burrito. I listened to a sermon on CD on my drive, and the minute I backed out of my parking space, I heard the preacher say, "I'll tell you why you're so confused . . . you're trying to figure everything out! You've got to leave some things alone and just trust God!" In only 10 minutes of driving, I got control over my thoughts and shut the devil up!

You can do the same thing! You can develop a habit of feeding your spirit the Truth in order to stay undeceived. There have been thousands of times (no exaggeration) when I have awakened from sleep experiencing mental anguish, anxiety, loneliness, temptations, sorrow, fear, you name it; and the minute I listened to a faith-building CD as I got ready to start my day, I have been impacted for the better. In the amount of time it took for me to put on my jogging clothes, brush my teeth, put a little (okay, a lot) of mascara on and some lipstick before going walking, I have heard things such as:

"Get a hold of yourself. Look yourself in the mirror and stop feeling sorry for yourself. You have Almighty God on the inside of you. The blood of Jesus runs through your veins. Stop letting a coward defeat you!"

"Quit letting your feelings make the decisions in your life. If you live by your feelings, you will be miserable!"

"Don't ever say again, 'I can't take anymore!' You can take anything the devil can dish out!"

"Every day is a proving day. Prove yourself today. Prove what you're made of!"

I love something pastor and author John Maxwell says. He says that if he could spend 24 hours with you to see what you do all day, he would be able to tell whether or not you will be successful. Based on your daily routine, he would be able to tell the direction your life is headed.

Well, if John Maxwell can tell where your life is going, based on your daily habits and decisions, don't you think God can? Unfortunately, the devil can too! Imagine as Satan is watching you open your eyes in the morning and the first thing out of your mouth is: "Praise You, Jesus. I love You, Jesus. I magnify You today!"

Then he sees you go in the bathroom and push "play" on your iPod or CD player, and the atmosphere is charged with faith-inspiring words like, "You have authority over Satan! God is on your side. God is hardening you to difficulty; and those things that used to destroy you and cause you to sink into a pit of destruction have lost their power over you! You're a child of the Most High God, and you can do all things through Christ who strengthens you!" You know what will happen? Hell will throw a temper tantrum. The devil hates to hear the Word of God preached.

Then it gets worse for him. Satan watches you go into another room in your house and lift your hands toward heaven. He's watching, he's cringing, he's confused, and he's wondering, "What is this child of God doing?" Then, he hears the most dreaded name of all. He hears you cry out, "JESUS, I submit my life unto You. I resist Satan and he must flee from me! Thank You for strengthening me, Lord. Thank You that the joy of the Lord is my strength! I magnify You for being my Deliverer and my Healer!"

Satan is going nuts. He's hoping this is just a one-time deal and it won't happen again. But it does. The next day and the next day and the next day. It's a lifestyle. It's a part of who you are. When you glorify God this way, life takes on a whole new meaning. You will look back and say, "I am not who I used to be."

I want you to know that *every single day* counts. Every time you pray, it changes things. Every time you sing to the Lord, it changes things. Every time you praise God under your breath to defeat tormenting thoughts, it changes things. Every act of obedience to God changes you and your circumstances.

5. Know What to Do, and Do It

If you want to fulfill God's plan for your life, you must do what you know God is telling you to do, not what He's telling others to do. What God is telling you to do may be completely different from what He is telling your friend to do or your husband or your children. You do what God's telling you to do . . . and keep it quiet.

I find that obeying God in the little things and keeping it between me and Him sure seems to make me feel closer to God and also boosts my confidence. It also proves that my obedience is purely out of love for God, not something I do to impress other people. That speaks volumes to God!

Determine that no matter what anyone else does, *you* will fulfill your assignment! Remember, you will be held accountable for your life, not someone else's life. You will answer for you! Don't look at the people around you. Do what you know YOU should be doing. You'll begin to demonstrate noticeable changes, and that will persuade them to want what you have!

If you know God's speaking to you today to start listening to His Word every single day, and you start doing that for one week, but then you look at your husband or your coworkers and notice they aren't doing it . . . that doesn't mean it's okay for you to quit!

There have been things that God has required of me to do in order to get free, and boy, oh boy, it seemed like so much. I would look around at other people and think, *Are you having to do all this?* But that wasn't the point. The point is that in order to be free and fulfill our unique plan in life, God will require us to do things that others aren't doing. Don't feel sorry for yourself. Don't think about it too much. Don't reason with God about it. Just do it.

God is the One you're listening to, so don't brag to others about how spiritual you are or how much God is requiring from you. Just do it and keep it between you and Him. It seems that God tends to reward that kind of obedience a lot sooner than later.

Do you want all of what God has for you or just 75 percent or 25 percent? Doing what God tells you to do will require living above the average. I heard someone say the other day, "Average is as close to the bottom as it is to the top." Do you want to be described as average? I'm sure you don't. Nobody wants to be average. Nobody likes being told they are average.

"How does she sing?" AVERAGE.

"How well does he write?" AVERAGE.

"How is her relationship with God?" AVERAGE.

"How is your marriage?" AVERAGE.

"How is your growth in God this year?" AVERAGE.

Being average is not anything to strive for. Being average won't change your life. Being average will keep you where you are. In order to stay focused on God's plan for your life, it will require doing more than others are willing to do. It will require not justifying why you can quit. It will require going the extra mile.

There are no traffic jams at the extra mile. Many folks are not willing to go the extra mile to break free from their past and fulfill God's unique assignment for them. They allow Satan to convince them that there is no unique assignment; it's just a pipe dream. They wallow in the pit of self-destruction by feeling sorry for themselves, giving Satan permission to torment their minds; and they complain that it's just too hard to shake those feelings. They yield to the temptations that surround them, concluding that's just who they are and there is no use fighting it!

Your breakthrough isn't dependent upon your hearing a brand-new solution every week. You just have to keep doing the right thing. The Bible tells us, "If you continue in my word, then are you my disciples indeed; and you shall know the truth, and the truth shall make you free" (John 8:31-32, *AKJV*). Continuing to do what we are supposed to do is the key to staying free.

By now, you have already proven that you are not a quitter. You have a desire deep on the inside of you to break free, to stay free and to walk free. The desire is already there, and that's enough to get you over the temptation of quitting! You have what it takes to be someone of influence. You have a testimony that could help young girls or young guys who are struggling with the very same issues. You have the wounds to prove that you fought and survived. You are here to testify that they can survive too!

Don't be average. Don't settle for whatever lies Satan is trying to feed your mind. Do what you know God is telling you to do, and do it with excellence! Go all the way! Do more than what is required. Double your efforts to get free. Listen to more faith-building messages than you did last month. Spend five more minutes a day in prayer. Fast a meal this week and spend that time in prayer. Confess a Scripture every single day this week. It will feed your faith and fuel your drive to live out God's destiny for your life.

You can do whatever God is telling you to do. You're not doing it in your own power or strength. You're doing it in God's strength coming on you. "He gives power to the weak, and to those who have no might He increases strength" (Isa. 40:29, *NKJV*). Don't take the lure that Satan is dangling in front of you. Lean on God's strength to get you through so you never have to be tempted to look back again!

Note
1. Mike Murdock, *101 Wisdom Keys* (Ft. Worth, TX: Perfect Publishing Mike Murdock Ministries, 1994).

7

WHEN THE SOUL TIES ARE PAINFUL... *YOUR PAIN WON'T LAST FOREVER*

If there's any chapter in this book that I have procrastinated writing, it is this one. Months have gone by in my life from the last chapter to this one because the subject matter is very sensitive. Though it is a difficult topic to address for many reasons, I included it because it is a big reason why many people are not letting go of their past. Some people can never fully move on or may find themselves "stuck" because they have not severed relationships with particular people that God wanted them to sever.

Could this be you? Perhaps you still dream about or long for someone that you were never able to release from your spirit, even though it's been years. Perhaps you are currently in an unhealthy relationship you know you should get out of. Perhaps you are in a sexual relationship with someone, and although you know it's wrong, you simply cannot resist the urge to be with that person.

What am I talking about? Soul ties.

Your soul is made up of your mind, your will and your emotions; it is your inner life. A soul tie is a connection that unites your internal being with another person. Soul ties are not necessarily bad. After all, God created them. They can be good if it's something that God wants for your life. As a matter of fact, in Matthew 18:19, Jesus says, "If two of you shall agree on earth as touching any thing that they shall ask, it shall be done for them" (*KJV*). When two people come together in a good soul tie, the power of God intensifies in you.

In 1 Samuel 18:1, we read that "the soul of Jonathan was knit to the soul of David" (*NKJV*). Jonathan's and David's souls were tied together in a way that God blessed. Likewise, marriage represents a good soul tie between a husband and wife, because their souls are joined together as one flesh (see Mark 10:8). Wrong soul ties, however, can negatively influence your faith journey. In 1 Corinthians 6:16, Paul warns of wrong "one flesh" unions—and therefore wrong soul ties—with prostitutes: "Do you not know that he who unites himself with a prostitute is one with her in body? For it is said, 'The two will become one flesh.'" If you feel tied to a person from your past that you cannot seem to break, you have a wrong soul tie.

As I headed out for my morning walk today, I saw my big dog, Chester Savoy Foy, tied to the gate. We are having some work done in our backyard and we didn't want Chester to get loose, so we had to tie him up. I visually saw him tied to the gate. He wasn't going anywhere. I was sure he wanted to. He desired to. He wished he could. But the fact is, that chain was pretty secure, and it kept him bound.

Think about your own life. What's keeping you bound? What are you tied to in your soul that you can't get free from? Who are you still emotionally connected to because of wrong soul ties? These chains must be broken.

If you have a wrong soul tie, you will not be at peace. If you are feeling in turmoil in a particular relationship, something is wrong. God has designed our good soul ties to make us feel good. Severing soul ties may be one of the most painful experiences in your life, but in order to carry out God's will for your life, it must be done. The good news is that the pain is temporary. It won't last forever. Severing a soul tie can bring you total freedom and transformation from your past.

How Soul Ties Are Formed

There are three ways soul ties are created.

1. Close Relationships

When you spend a lot of time with someone, you are forming a bond. Through whatever you do together—eating, traveling, working, talking—the connection strengthens. You have soul ties with your coworkers, your family members, your children, your classmates.

In the Bible, we see that King David and his buddy Jonathan had a good soul tie as a direct result of a healthy friendship: "And it came to pass, when he had made an end of speaking unto Saul, that the soul of Jonathan was knit with the soul of David, and Jonathan loved him as his own soul" (1 Sam. 18:1, *KJV*).

Jonathan was the legal heir to the throne of Saul, but God chose David to be king. Though that may have been a recipe for jealousy, God enabled Jonathan to love David so much that he, of his own will, allowed David to have what belonged to him. This friendship lasted even beyond the grave. When Jonathan died, David looked for relatives of Jonathan that he could bless for Jonathan's sake.

This is a perfect example of a God-designed soul tie. In this type of kinship, God's power increases. The same is true for a wrong soul tie. In that instance, it opens an opportunity for

Satan to work on your behalf, and his evil power is intensified.

I have a soul tie with my best friend, Theresa. We have been best friends since 1985. The years have been filled with a lot of tears, laughter, hard times, learning times, fun and challenges. We feel like we've been through it all together. I cannot imagine my life without Theresa. She has been such a pillar of strength to me. I can tell her anything in the world and she still loves me, believes in me and trusts me. We have a good soul tie.

When my husband and I were youth pastors, we formed soul ties with the youth department. We spent hundreds of hours with those precious teenagers. We led many of them to the Lord; we prayed with them, played sand volleyball with them and helped many of them through tough times. We actually built the youth building with our personal money. We poured our heart and soul into this ministry. When the time came for us to resign, it literally tore me apart inside. Why? Because of these soul ties.

I can remember the first Wednesday night that someone else was going to teach "our" teens. I couldn't even drive by the church building because it hurt too badly. When my husband and I were invited to visit one night, I cried the whole service. It was "my" building, "my" teenagers, "my" vision. Now all those things were different. It all belonged to someone else. They were not mine. Though it was the will of God that these new pastors lead the youth, it still hurt. See, you can be in the perfect will of God and still be pained inside when the time comes to sever soul ties from your past.

Having close relationships and forming soul ties with people through friendships is a good thing; however, close relationships that aren't pleasing to God are a huge detriment to your life. Any close relationship that is pulling you out of God's will for your life is a wrong soul tie. Anyone who does not respect your desire to please God should not be an influence in your life. I read this quote once, and it has stayed with me: "Anyone who does not respect your assignment disqualifies himself (herself) from a close relationship."

There are some people you could be tied to; and now, in order for you to move on with your life, you know that you must let go. Don't stop reading this book because you think it will hurt too much. Keep reading and I'll show you how God can get you through.

2. Vows, Commitments and Promises

Soul ties can be formed by the words of your mouth. Words have such power over your life! Think of what it really means when you say statements such as: "I will never stop loving you." "You will always be the only one I love." "I will never get you out of my heart." "You're the only one I will ever give my love to." "Nobody will ever take your place in my life." Can you just imagine how much power these words yield?

The Bible says that we can be "snared" by the words of our mouth: "You are snared by the words of your mouth; you are taken by the words of your mouth" (Prov. 6:2, *NKJV*). A snare means a trap, a hook, a plan. Your very own words could be keeping you trapped to a bad soul tie, which explains why you feel like something is pulling on you, preventing you from fully going forward.

You may be doing everything you know to do to break free from an old relationship, but something keeps pulling on you. How could that be? Words. The things you said to this person, no matter how long ago you said them, still carry some weight. And unless you get rid of that weight, you will be dragging it with you into the future.

How did God create the world? Through His words. If you read through the first couple of chapters of Genesis, you can clearly see how God spoke the entire world into existence. He said it, and it happened. He set the example that we can create a "world" with what comes out of our mouths.

Think about a wedding ceremony. A minister asks you to verbally answer the question as to whether or not you want to marry your future spouse. Your words create the marital covenant.

I've always known the power of words because of the faith-filled home I grew up in. To say something like, "That makes me sick," was the equivalent of cussing. But I never thought about vows, promises or commitments as being used as a snare in my life. As I began to look at the soul ties of my past and search for why I still felt "snared" or "held captive" to old memories and painful experiences, I remembered many words exchanged between me and other people.

I've studied this topic for my own freedom and have realized that I needed to take authority over the words I spoke in the past.

I know you can't remember every single vow, promise or commitment you made, but I do believe if you are serious about this, God will bring specific things to your mind. If you want to break wrong soul ties, you must recognize the power of your words.

3. Sexual Relationships

Soul ties are formed any time and every time there is intimacy in a relationship. Sex tightens soul ties and makes it so much harder to cut the ties when you try to stop. Godly soul ties are formed when a married couple engages in sexual intercourse. It is the way God designed it (see Mark 10:8). Ungodly soul ties are formed when unmarried people have sex. You may have ended a physically intimate relationship months ago, but you still feel a pull toward that person. Why? Because of soul ties.

When we give ourselves sexually to another person, a part of our soul is chipped away. When we give ourselves to many sexual partners, many pieces of our soul are chipped away. Eventually, we will feel like one fragmented person incapable of loving just one person fully and completely. Something blocks us from giving our whole selves to one person, perhaps even our marriage partner, because we aren't a whole person. Our soul is still tied, to some degree, to the people we've been intimate with.

Let's say that you have had three sexual partners before you get married. You can't give 100 percent of yourself to your marriage partner because 75 percent of you is still tied to other people. Unless those soul ties have been broken, you are only capable of giving 25 percent of yourself. Nearly half (46 percent) of all 15-

to 19-year-olds in America have had sex at least once. By age 19, 7 in 10 never-married teens have engaged in sexual intercourse.[1] It's no wonder we have so many divorces. Our marriages can't be whole until our pasts are dealt with before God.

Sex before marriage, among Christian men and women, is more common than we even realize. In the numerous conferences, workshops and church services where I have shared my story of getting pregnant out of wedlock, I meet so many girls who love God and are having sex with their boyfriends. When I was in college, taking an elective on "Courtship and Marriage" (it was an easy *A*, okay), the entire class participated in an anonymous sex survey. The study was conducted purely for compiling data.

The survey was very blunt and, quite frankly, embarrassing. Everybody was trying to make sure no other person could see what they were writing down. I even swung my long hair over my paper to make sure only I could see the paper. Here were some of the questions asked:

- Are you a virgin?
- How old were you when you lost your virginity?
- Was it a one-night stand or did you date?
- How many sexual partners have you had?
- How old are you?
- Do you have sex on the first date?
- How far will you go on a first date? (with a list of multiple choices)
- Do you have oral sex?
- Would you have oral sex on the first date?

The questions went on and on. The next day, our professor revealed this startling fact. Among 500 students who took the survey that day, there were only six virgins. Looking back, it is very shocking; that meant there were 494 broken students who were bound with ungodly soul ties.

It has been said that sexual sins are the most painful and that they require the longest amount of time to recover from than any other sin. When we engage in sex outside of the marriage covenant, we actually sin against our own body. "He who commits sexual immorality sins against his own body" (1 Cor. 6:18, *NKJV*).

Sexual soul ties prevent us from moving on to new relationships, even the ones God may be leading us into. This can even happen in situations of divorce. The divorce is over, a new marriage is pursued, but one spouse keeps being drawn back to her or his ex-husband or ex-wife. Their soul is still tied to the former spouse.

James 1:8 says, "A double minded man is unstable in all his ways" (*KJV*). A double-minded person has a divided soul. Do you feel unstable at times? Do you want to move on with life but are struck in random moments of missing your ex-boyfriend? This is being double-minded and is not something God wants you to experience.

God does not want your soul fragmented. He does not want you longing for a past that He has delivered you from. He wants you free from every sin of your past—even the ones you willfully gave into over and over but still think about.

My Story

Because of the power that wrong soul ties had on me, there was a point in my life when I could not break free from an abusive relationship. My friends could clearly point out how insane it was for me to stay with this particular guy. They would tell me, "Terri, wake up! You're crazy if you stay with him! Don't let him treat you like this!" And guess what? I would stay with him.

We were in love. We spent nearly three years dating each other. We spent almost every waking minute together. We talked about our future. We talked about marriage and kids. We spent Christmas and Thanksgiving holidays with each other's families. We exchanged gifts. We had romantic picnics by the lake. We went to the movies. We had dinners at every restaurant in Fort Worth. We voiced our love for each other. We couldn't imagine anyone else in our lives. We were intimate with each other. We had strong soul ties.

Then the relationship became abusive. Our bond was so tight that if any other guy hugged me or looked at me the wrong way, my boyfriend became furious. One day his jealousy escalated into a physical attack. We had just finished dinner at our favorite restaurant, and in the middle of our conversation, during the meal, his jealousy arose. Rather than just end the date and take me home, he wanted to talk in the car in the restaurant parking lot. I said okay.

In a few minutes, he grabbed my neck and started banging my head against the steering wheel of his car. I thought I was dreaming. I couldn't believe the person I loved so much would do this to me. *I don't deserve this! I have to get away from him!* I thought to myself.

But before he dropped me off at my house, he started gushing with apologies. Tears flowed down his face, and he kept saying, "I'm sorry." Through his disbelief, he embraced me and said, "Terri, I can't believe I did that to you. You're so precious to me. I love you. I will never hurt you again. How could I have done that? You're the one I love more than anyone in the world." Soul ties kept us together even after that incident.

As you probably suspect, the abuse of that night wasn't the only time it ever happened. In fact, the attacks intensified. The abuse continued, from being dragged by my neck in a parking lot to being thrown on the ground and choked. But I remained in denial. I justified the abuse. I forgave. I hoped it would never happen again. I hid every bit of it from my parents and friends. I believed his words, his sorrow and his tears. Why? Soul ties.

Every now and then I would muster up the courage to leave him, but it wasn't more than a matter of days before we were back together again. This went on for a long time. After one of the worst events, I finally developed the strength to completely end the relationship. I left him for good. Months later, I ran into him, and seeing him just crushed my heart. I missed him. I wanted him. I could only remember the good times.

Those soul ties were strong. Satan knows the power of soul ties, especially in abusive relationships. It typically takes an abused woman about seven attempts to leave her abuser for good. Some never make it.

Breaking Soul Ties

I know it's especially difficult and painful when you break soul ties of a recent relationship. Because this person is very much alive in your heart, you cannot even comprehend life without him or her at this minute. These ties are not only firmly wrapped around you, but they have dead bolts and padlocks on them so strong they seem to be saying, "You're never breaking free . . . ever!" Just the thought of letting go feels like you're being stripped of your ability to breathe. Trust me, I know. I've been there. When I had to let go of my soul ties, I was so consumed with anxiety that I couldn't eat or sleep.

There are certain things you can do to help you through this trying and uncomfortable process of breaking free from a relationship you feel God wants you to get free of.

Decide to Please God More than Anyone Else

You have one life to live, and it matters to God. One day, you will stand before God and give an account of your life and what you were called to do during your time here on earth. You cannot live your life displeasing God in order to please someone else. All that will do is eventually bring you a life of deep regret.

You can get so close to people that you become more interested in doing what they want you to do rather than what God wants you to do. You may live in fear of someone being mad at you if you don't give in to his or her demands. Maybe you don't want to appear mean or hurtful, so you continue to let the person control you and manipulate you. This behavior must stop.

You have to come to the place in your life where pleasing God is the most important thing to you. If He is prompting you to end a relationship that you're tied to, then you need to end it. If you are having ungodly contact with someone to whom you are not married, STOP. If you're having sex with someone outside of marriage, STOP. If you are befriending someone who doesn't support your faith, STOP. Don't go another day without making these right decisions. Don't justify wrong soul ties. Your future is at stake.

Allowing someone to have as much influence as God should have in your life opens the door for Satan to come into your life. He will make it so much harder for you to give up this soul tie. The right time to cut the strings is now. Today. Even this very minute.

You cannot allow a person to be a god or an idol in your life. An idol is anyone you have assigned to be to you what only God can be to you. For example, only God can be your comforter, your healer, your deliverer, your safety and your savior. Your husband, your boyfriend, your best friend, your mother—none of these persons can act in those roles. God is a jealous God and will not share your devotion with another.

Once you've been intimate with someone, and you decide to stop, it will not be an easy road to travel. The warm and fuzzy feelings will surface and you'll just naturally want to yield to them. This is why you cannot make and live out this decision on your own. You must choose God over people and your feelings. Trust Him, and I promise you, He will see you through.

Build Yourself Up in the Word

You must have *daily* doses of God's Word in order to develop the strength to sever an ungodly soul tie. Reading, studying and memorizing Scripture is what builds up your spirit and gives you strength. Filling yourself with God's Word can help you make the right decisions. It must be a part of your strategic plan to be free of your past.

The Bible is our greatest weapon against Satan. He does not want you to break your soul ties. He is desperately working to keep you locked into this situation. The devil will lie to you and convince you that you cannot live without your ungodly soul tie. He will remind you of all the good times, the fun times, the romantic times, the giddy times. He'll torment you day and night into thinking you cannot live without this person.

The devil is a liar.

God's Word, the Truth, will override Satan's lies. Just like anything else, however, you won't see results overnight. Repeating Bible verses for a few days won't necessarily keep Satan at bay for the next month. You have to make studying the Word a habit. Do it every day. Don't stop. God rewards persistence.

Wean Yourself from that Ungodly Soul Tie

You literally have to wean yourself from that person to whom you have an ungodly soul tie. To wean means to deprive. You have to deprive yourself of this lover, boyfriend or friend until you no longer miss him or her. Mark my words: There *will* come a day when you will no longer miss that person. At this stage, you may feel that completely letting go of him or her just isn't possible. But be encouraged, the more you devote your energies to severing this soul tie, the more the person will be completely cut off from your life.

Let me explain how to wean yourself the way I learned it from Joyce Meyer. Psalm 131:2 tells us, "Surely I have calmed and quieted my soul, like a weaned child with his mother; like a weaned child is my soul within me [ceased from fretting]" (*AMP*). I remember when I was trying to wean my daughter from the pacifier. Every night it had become a a part of our nightly routine after I nursed her to put a pacifier in her mouth to help her fall asleep for the night. An hour or two later, I would remove the pacifier, and her little mouth would still be moving as if the pacifier were still there! It was so cute.

However, when it was time to wean her from it, it was torture. It was unbearable for her and she screamed at the top of her lungs for the rubbery object; and it was unbearable for me as I could not do anything except let her cry. Oh, it broke my heart. I kept telling my husband, "I should just go in there and give her the stupid pacifier already." He refused to let me do it and said, "No, Terri, just let her cry or else you'll have to go through this again. She'll eventually stop." I think it was harder on me than for my little girl. I felt like a bad mom! Finally, what felt like an eternity of torturing my baby finally ended. She cried herself to sleep.

The next night, it didn't get any easier! It was like starting over again. She sobbed and screamed for what she was used to getting. The same thing happened the next night and the one after that. One night, however, the crying seemed to fade. It wasn't as loud or as long as the previous nights. Eventually, of course, the crying completely stopped. The hours of crying turned into nights of silence. My baby stopped missing her pacifier.

When you first deny yourself of your wrong soul tie, rest assured that your spirit will throw a fit. Your emotions will scream and fight for the right to stay in bondage. But the more you deny yourself the thing that you are screaming for, the less you begin to desire it. Your flesh will eventually stop throwing temper tantrums and will start being subsided by the Spirit of God.

Jesus reminded us of the principle of saying no to our sinful selves, our flesh: "If anyone decides to come after Me, *let him deny himself* [forget, ignore, disown, and lose sight of himself and his own interests]" (Mark 8:34, *AMP*, emphasis added).

Sometimes our desire to keep that person around can lead toward addictive behaviors. We can actually become addicted to people. An addiction is anything you have to have in order to feel settled inside. It's where your mind won't stop racing, your emotions are raging and your flesh is going haywire if you don't get your craving met.

Don't give in to the addiction. Deny yourself that person. The pain and the cravings will go away. It may not be in a week, a month or even a year; but if you persevere, one day you will wake up and the desperate feelings you had to hold on to the person will have vanished.

There are many ways to wean yourself off of an ungodly soul tie. The most obvious and important action to take is to cut all communication. Don't call the person. Don't answer their phone calls. Don't hang out in places where you know they'll be. Don't be alone with them. Don't email them. Delete their emails. You may have to take drastic measures to be free, but I promise you, it's worth it. Doing this is being obedient to God, and you will never regret submitting to your heavenly Father.

As bad as it may hurt right now to not keep that ungodly soul tie, remember that you are not rejecting that person; you are rejecting sin! That's a big difference! Satan will make you feel guilty by telling you how mean you are for "rejecting" that person. "How can you be so cold? How can you be so cruel? How could you hurt someone you made love to? How could you reject someone who truly loves you?" These are lies. You are not saying no to that person; you are saying no to sin. And that pleases God.

Clean Out Your House

Yes, you need to do some serious cleaning out. Whatever items or memorabilia you may have lying around that are connected to your ungodly soul tie must go in the trash. You probably have no idea of what keeping those things around is doing to your emotional wellbeing. They keep you tied to your past.

Satan works against us through our five physical senses: sight, hearing, touch, taste and smell. He uses these channels to tempt us with certain things. Think about it. All it takes is one whiff of an old boyfriend's cologne, and suddenly the old feelings come back and you start to miss him terribly. That one smell that is so familiar to you can send you into a tailspin straight to your past.

I remember an old boyfriend once bought me a teddy bear that he drenched in his cologne. I slept with that stuffed animal every night just so I could be reminded of him. Though that happened so many years ago, I sometimes think of him when I pass another man wearing that very same fragrance.

You can listen to a song that reminds you of your soul tie. You can watch a movie that reminds you of your soul tie. A certain color can even remind you of your soul tie. Satan knows this and will use whatever he can to get you thinking about your soul tie. This is why it's so important for you to walk around your house and throw out anything that reminds you of this person.

You need to schedule a special clean-up and clean-out day. Go through every room, every closet, every drawer and every cabinet. Throw away anything that has a negative emotional tie to it. There may be things you can sell such as jewelry that you don't need to hang on to. There may be old movies that you don't need to watch or old CDs you don't need to listen to. You can take those to certain stores and sell them. Hey, make some money off of it at the same time you're gaining more freedom from your past! I did.

I didn't finish my cleaning out in a day or a week. It was a lengthy process. I have to admit there were certain things I did not want to throw away on the first go-around. I just couldn't bring myself to completely toss it all out. This made me realize that I wasn't ready to completely let go of certain things. I needed to get more aggressive about this thing. I prayed more, listened to the Word more and got more excited about the new things

God wanted to do in my life. I just had to throw everything out if I wanted to experience the kind of future God had planned for my life.

I'm not saying that everything connected to your past has to be trashed or that every single picture of you and an old flame has to be destroyed. I still have some photos of high school and college boyfriends. I'm just saying that anything that has a hold on you in some way and is keeping you from total freedom needs to be cleared out of your life. These could be pictures, letters, emails, gifts, clothing, CDs, DVDs, you name it. They need to go.

Cleaning up your house, or in the grand scheme of things, your life, may seem like extreme behavior, but you need to do it. You don't need to cling to the past. You will not regret throwing these things out. I'm telling you from personal experience that you don't need them. If you want to have freedom from the past, throw out the past.

I learned some powerful Scriptures to help me get through this activity:

I will set nothing wicked before my eyes (Ps. 101:3, *NKJV*).

Do not bring a detestable thing into your house or you, like it, will be set apart for destruction (Deut. 7:26, *NIV*).

I will walk within my house with a perfect heart (Ps. 101:2, *NJKV*).

Memorize these passages to help you understand the importance of getting rid of wrong soul ties. Remember, when one thing ends, God begins something new.

Break the Power of Your Words

As I mentioned earlier, I did not realize how powerful my words were in keeping my soul tied to another person. I had become "snared" by the words of my mouth, and I had to break the power of my words to escape it. As the psalmist writes, "We have escaped like a bird out of the fowler's snare; the snare has been broken, and we have escaped" (Ps. 124:7, *NIV*).

It's imperative that you take authority over the words you have spoken that may have created an unhealthy or ungodly connection with someone. How do you do that? You can simply ask God to bring specific vows and promises to your remembrance. Or you can simply say with a repentant and sincere heart, "Father, in the name of Jesus, I renounce all promises, vows and ungodly words spoken by me or agreement with someone else that have kept me in bondage to my past. I take authority over those words in Jesus' name and break the power of them over my life."

I close this chapter by saying that I am so proud of you. Even though you may not have done what this chapter is challenging you to do, you are taking a step in the right direction by reading it. This proves that you want to be free even though it will hurt. Dear reader, you can do it. You can break free from anyone who has an ungodly hold on you. I pray that you will listen to God speaking quietly to your spirit and not justify why it seems to be okay for you to stay attached to your soul tie. If God is nudging you inside to break free, submit to that nudge. Heed the voice of God. Follow His leading.

I think sometimes we're so afraid of hurting when we do let go that we prolong the closure to the past. I have learned that the peace and joy I have after I let go far surpass the pain of cutting ties. When you compromise, agony and anxiety become your companions. When you obey God, peace and joy become a part of your life. You can never have total peace when you're in disobedience to God. The only way to obtain peace is to submit to Him and do whatever He wants you to do.

Feelings lie. You have to shut them up and do what you know you're supposed to do. You can't do it on your own. If you could, it wouldn't require God! Lean on Him like never before. Know that you are not alone. God is right there with you, ready and willing to take you by the hand and walk you through this. Cry out to Him. Build yourself up in the Word. Listen to what He is saying. Hear how He wants to change your life and give you the freedom to live life His way—the best way.

You may have tried to break free once before and were not able to. Don't be discouraged. It doesn't mean this time won't work. Don't make the assumption that, because you couldn't do it before, you'll never be able to.

This brings to mind a story I heard about an elephant that was tied to an 18-inch stake at a circus. Do you think this gigantic elephant was strong enough to break free from a measly stick in the ground? Of course he was! But he had tried to when he was a baby and wasn't able to. Years later, he determined there was no point in even trying again. So there he was, this massive creature capable of pulling down trees, held captive by a puny stake.

What stake is holding you back? What stake could faith break you free from? However strong that stake is in your life, it is nowhere near as powerful as God. What may have defeated you years ago doesn't have to keep you defeated.

One of my favorite Bible verses that helped me through rough times in my life is found in Isaiah 49. Anytime you find yourself going back to an ungodly soul tie, read this verse. My prayer is that it will sustain you and keep you from going back where you don't belong.

I have chosen you and not cast you off [even though you are exiled]. Fear not [there is nothing to fear], for I am with you; do not look around you in terror and be dismayed, for I am your God. I will strengthen and harden you to difficulties, yes, I will help you; yes, I will hold you up and retain you with My [victorious] right hand of rightness and justice (Isa. 41:9-10, *AMP*).

Note

1. J. C. Abama, G. M. Martinez, B. S. Dawson, et al, "Teenagers in the United States: Sexual Activity, Contraceptive Use, and Childbearing, 2002," *Vital and Health Statistics*, series 23, no. 24, December 2004. www.cdc.gov/nchs/data/series/sr_23/sr23_024.pdf.

8

WHEN YOU LET GO OF YOUR PAST...*YOUR CALLING WILL BE CALLING*

If you don't know where you're headed, then any road will take you there.
DOROTHY, IN *THE WIZARD OF OZ*

I began this book by urging you to get a vision for your life and write your own obituary. I must close out this book the same way. If there's anything that has aided me in my quest to be free from the past, it has been to dream big and have a vision to stay focused on every day. Even now, today, my vision is what gets me up in the morning; it helps me resist temptations and avoid distractions; it makes me enjoy living and feel that I have a purpose.

I said it before and I'll say it again: A person with no vision will always return to his or her past. Your vision will keep you from what you don't want to return to: past habits, past relationships, past fears, past insecurities, past mindsets, past addictions, past behaviors and past thinking.

You might be saying, "Terri, I've read the whole book now, and I still don't know my vision." I understand. I didn't know what mine was for a long time. As a young woman, my biggest vision was to be a Dallas Cowboys cheerleader! Once I gave up that dream, I wondered what God wanted me to do. Maybe teach French? Ghostwrite for people? Be a youth pastor or a stay-at-home mom? I was very confused.

As Stephen Covey puts it, "Begin with the end in mind." It wasn't until I thought in terms of writing my own obituary that I realized how I wanted people to remember me and began walking toward it. As I stated in chapter 4, it was in my *daily routine* of seeking God that I discovered more and more of God's plan. It wasn't a one-time supernatural visitation from God; it was a process.

Fulfilling your destiny is not the result of one big event. It's a result of daily habits and choices that lead you to realize God's overall plan. Experts say that if you commit one hour a day for five years to a particular subject, you can become an "expert" in that field. If you have not already done so, go back to the chapter challenge for chapter 4 and apply some daily goal-setting in the six areas you want to focus on every day (use my six areas as a reference, if needed). Do this for 21 days without stopping. After that amount of time, you are ready to make focusing on your vision a habit.

I am telling you the truth: I did not have a clue that I would ever preach, write books, minister on television, or have my own website. I didn't even have a desire to do any of these things. It was through pursuing a daily goal to spend time with God, hear the Word and write down what I heard that I began to realize my dreams. Your daily vision will lead to discovering your overall vision for life.

Don't Waste More Time

Remember the vision I had of being handed a clipboard and some keys? I was told that it was an assignment on my life. I want you to view your life as an assignment from God. I want you to see your name on a clipboard with a to-do list attached to it. Not only that, but I want you to realize that you have a deadline. You have a time frame in which you are to complete your assignment. You don't have any more time to waste!

Perhaps, up to now, you have felt like Isaiah did when he wrote, "I have labored to *no purpose*; I have spent my strength in vain and for nothing" (Isa. 49:4, *NIV*, emphasis added). I know that I have felt that way. Those writings sound like my old journals! But not anymore. My prayer is that you will see your time on earth as precious and priceless, and that you will determine to make every day count. How much time do you have left? Every day is another day recorded in history that you no longer have to live. I'm not saying that to scare you; I'm saying it to motivate you to get moving.

David wrote, "LORD, remind me how brief my time on earth will be. Remind me that my days are numbered—how fleeting my life is" (Ps. 39:4, *NLT*). Later he said, "I am here on earth for just a little while" (Ps. 119:19, *TEV*). When you die, there will most likely be a tombstone with your full name on it. Also engraved on that tombstone will be your birth date and the date that you died. It's that little *dash* in the middle that determines what you did with your life. That little dash represents how you lived—whether you fulfilled God's plan for your life or fulfilled Satan's plan.

Walk around a cemetery sometime and look at all the gravestones. It makes you wonder, *Did they answer the call? Did they doubt God's calling? Did they allow their past to prevent them from going forward? Did they die with their dreams never realized? Did they make some-*

thing of their lives? Did they make God smile? Did they live here for a purpose or just live? Did they fulfill God's assignment for them?

Ask yourself these questions right now. Are you answering the call? Are you doubting God's calling? Are you allowing your past to prevent you from moving forward? Use these questions as a barometer to gauge where you are on the road to your future.

Answer the Call

In my quiet time with God one day, I heard these words in the depths of my spirit: "Your calling is calling!" Then I heard, "Now lead them into theirs." As you near the end of this book, I pray that I have done my job. I pray that you are being led out of your past and into an amazing future.

God is calling you. He's calling your name. He wants you to answer His calling and do what He has assigned you to do. You may have ignored God's calling on your life for so long that you no longer hear the call anymore. You may have listened to other voices for so long that you doubt what it is that God wants you to do. I am praying that today will be a new beginning in your life.

Don't let your *past* keep you from answering the call.

Don't let *other people* keep you from answering the call.

Don't let *finances* keep you from answering the call.

Don't let *past failures* keep you from answering the call.

Don't let *Satan* talk you out of answering the call.

Don't let *"busy-ness"* keep you from answering the call.

Don't let *shame and guilt* keep you from answering the call.

Don't let *insecurity* keep you from answering the call.

Your Decisions Matter

You can choose to either ignore God's calling or pursue it. Your decision will affect the rest of your life. Everything you do today—every decision you make, every thought you have, every action in which you engage—will have a result somewhere down the line. Not only do your decisions affect your life, but they also affect those around you.

I can't help but think about my dad's decision to surrender His life to the Lord back in 1969. His one decision altered *my* life forever . . . and the lives of countless others. When my dad answered the call to the ministry, he moved our family from Shreveport, Louisiana, to Fort Worth, Texas. If he hadn't done that, would I be serving God today? Would I be living in Texas? Would I have gone to Texas Tech University? Would I be married to Rodney? Because I grew up in Texas, I met my husband at Texas Tech University. Because my dad was in the ministry, I began working for him, which eventually led to launching my own ministry, which led to writing this book, which led to your reading it.

One decision.

Your decision to move forward into the future with God's plan matters. Just as a good decision will affect you and future generations, so will a bad decision. What kind of decisions? A decision to leave when you should have stayed; a decision to get back into drugs; a decision to drink a little alcohol here and there; a decision to not go to church; a decision to quit your job; a decision to not step out into a new line of work when your family is suffering financially; a decision to leave your wife for another woman or leave your husband for another man. All of these decisions will affect your destiny and the destiny of those around you.

T. D. Jakes has said, "The decisions you make today are going to be the path to your destiny. There is a correlation between your decisions and your destiny. If your decisions don't start lining up with your destiny, you will spend your life going in circles." Decide today that you will pick up the call and pursue God's plan for your life.

First Things First

"How do you eat an elephant?" Well, personally, I don't eat elephants, but the answer is "one bite at a time." How do you go after this big vision for your life? One day at a time.

When you pursue your vision one day at a time, one of the habits that will help you be successful is the ability to prioritize. You must be able to prioritize your daily routine. As Stephen Covey, author of *The 7 Habits of Highly Successful People*, states it, "Put first things first." What should your biggest priority be? *Spending time alone with God.* Think of this time just like you think of breakfast, lunch or dinner. You wouldn't forget to eat, right? Well, you shouldn't forget to spend time with your Creator. Doing this will give you the greatest return on your investment. If you want to fulfill the very purpose for which you were born, you have to make time with God the number-one priority of your life!

I know that I have shared this with you throughout the book, but it's been said that "priorities never stay put." Satan is after your time with God. Unfortunately, it's usually the first thing to go when we get busy or life seems relatively carefree. Sometimes when we are not suffering or going through trying situations, we tend to put God on the backburner. Don't let that happen to you.

Spending time with the Lord is THE VERY THING that has brought the most healing to my life. It has brought me confidence. It has brought me peace. It has brought me healing. It has brought me restoration.

In the Bible, when Jesus was baptized in the Jordan River, and the Holy Spirit came upon Him in the form of a dove, He did not immediately go out and perform miracles and signs and wonders in front of large crowds. What did He do? He went to the wilderness alone to fast and pray . . . by Himself. He had to spend alone time with God, fasting and praying, before He ever stepped out into His ministry. We need to do the same thing. Making God our top priority is what leads us into the future He has created for us.

Preparation Is Key

Now that you know your number-one priority, *time with God,* what are you going to do right now to prepare for what you believe God has called you to do? I ought to be able to look around your house and see where your life is headed.

How would I determine that? By looking at these areas: What kind of books are you reading? What kind of CDs are you listening to? Where is most of your money going? Are you researching your dream? Are you attending a class? Are you saving money for it? What are you doing to prepare for your life assignment?

Preparation takes effort! Any successful person you know got to that place because he or she prepared for it. They had a plan and took the steps to execute that plan. You can have a Bible on your nightstand, but if you never take the time to read it, it won't do you any good. You may live close to a bookstore or library, but if you have never read one book that relates to where you want your future to go, nothing will change.

Obviously, you care about your future or you wouldn't be reading this book right now. You have proven that if you want to succeed, you have to invest in your future. Your action words are "learn," "grow," "expand your thinking," "prepare."

Success isn't something you arrive at; it's something you prepare for! You have to take the time to read, study, learn and grow one day at a time. I remember the first time I went to a Youth Pastors' Conference where thousands of youth pastors were in attendance. The guest speakers were so knowledgeable and quoted famous people left and right. They never stammered; they were confident in their speaking and sounded very articulate. To be honest, I felt a little insecure and definitely overwhelmed. It seemed hopeless that I would ever be as smooth as they were.

You may feel the same way when you look at other people who are doing what you want to do. You may wonder, *Where do I even start?* I discovered that you start with one book . . . one day. When you finish that book, you move on to another one. It starts with listening to one faith-building CD one morning. And when you're done, you move on to another one.

Your calling won't just happen. It won't just fall into your lap one afternoon. You have to pursue it on purpose and do whatever you need to do to get there. It may be a long and hard road, but don't get discouraged. God can accelerate things in your life, but you have to at least put your foot on the gas pedal.

Picture Your Dreams on Paper

There is something God wants you to do during your time here on earth, and He's going to hold you accountable for it! A few years ago, I heard the Lord say, "When I know you're ready, get ready!" I wasn't sure what that meant, but I knew I needed to devote more time to getting my vision/my dreams on paper and preparing myself to go after them.

So, I revisited my "obituary" (my dreams for the future) that I had written two years before and recalled something I wrote. It said, "Who knew that a little redhead from Texas, speaking rusty French, would make such an impact on a nation. Terri made a difference in the nation of France with the love of Jesus." Keep in mind that when I wrote that, I didn't even know a soul in Paris, France! I didn't have anybody asking me to preach. I didn't have any teaching material in French. I didn't even have any plans to go to France. But I wrote those words anyway.

I have a degree in French, and I love the French people. But what do I do with that? Where do I start? I started by sowing seed into a church in Paris where my dad preached. I gave my personal money to the pastors of this great church because of the impact they were already making in France.

Every dream I've seen come to pass in my life has required that I sow a seed toward it. If you want apple trees in your backyard, you can't just wish for them or hope they'll appear one day or speak to the ground and command the apple tree to appear! You have to sow a seed for it. It's the same with the dreams God has for your life. You must sow toward those dreams.

You've probably heard the phrase, "What you make happen for others, God will make happen for you." When you get involved in sowing toward someone else's dreams, God will send people to sow into your dreams. I've seen it happen over and over again.

The book you are reading right now is the result of a dream. I applied the very steps that I am teaching you. I sowed seed into another author who writes Christian books that I love to read, and I was believing God for a publisher for my first book. I began writing the book, finished it and I was ready when the publisher called.

When you get involved in the dreams of others, God will get involved in yours!

Then I bought a map of France and framed it in my office. I put the vision in front of me, not to mention that I have Eiffel Towers all over my office and home!

I began to think and pray *daily* about what God would want me to do. The idea came to me to write a mini-book in French and pass it out all over France. So, I decided to start where I was and I began writing a book for the people of France.

I scheduled time in the mornings to devote at least one hour to write two days a week. One Saturday morning, I penciled in my calendar, "Write French book from 7:00–9:00." And I kept the commitment.

Habbakuk 2:2 says, "Write the vision and make it plain on tablets . . . for the vision is yet for an appointed time" (*NKJV*). You have to appoint a time to go after your dreams!

Instead of just waiting for someone to call me and say, "Can you preach in Paris this year?" I began preparing for the dream. I wrote the mini-book in less than two weeks, and I believed God for an opportunity to preach in Paris so that I could distribute this book all over the city.

Since writing the book, God supernaturally brought people into my life who donated finances for the printing! In other words, where there's vision, there's always *provision*! God is so amazing! We got the books printed and ready to go!

You can imagine what happened next: I received two invitations to preach in churches in the city of Paris! In other words, *"When I know you're ready, get ready."*

Picture yourself in your dreams! In other words, what do you see yourself doing . . . what do you see yourself being? You've got to see something before you can build something!

When Rodney and I were building our house, we met with the builder that first time, and he said, "What do you see?" I just sat there. I didn't have a clue. Rodney had some ideas about what he wanted, but I didn't. I hadn't spent any time thinking about it, dreaming about it, planning it. I was so *busy* with work and life that it wasn't at the forefront of my mind. Did you get that? *I didn't devote time to planning my dream.* I wanted to just buy a house already built and move in!

The builder said, "You need to drive around and look at houses and get ideas. Take pictures of what you like and show me." It took time out of my busy schedule to do it. There were times when Rodney would say, "We'd better go drive around." But we had just gotten off work and didn't feel like doing it. Sometimes I did and sometimes I didn't.

In fact, I have discovered that the timing of our dreams is pretty much up to us. How diligent are we about pursuing the dream? In our case, we delayed our own dream house by not being ready! Which dreams are you delaying by not being ready? Do you have a plan? What do you see (inside)?

Finally, we took the time to drive around neighborhood after neighborhood and took pictures of the houses we liked. It was a start! We showed the builder the pictures. But we still weren't ready. He said, "Look in magazines; get ideas of what style you like." He was so patient with us. He even said, "If I didn't like you so much, I would have told y'all to leave a long time ago." Why? We weren't ready. We didn't have a picture in our minds of what we wanted our dream house to be.

Every dream, every goal, every vision starts with a picture. You have to picture yourself in your dreams!

Albert Einstein said, "Your imagination is a preview of life's coming attractions." If you don't have a picture in your mind of what you want to do with your life, then you're just doing busy-work. You're just killing time. You're just existing. That is not God's best for your life.

I'm not saying you have to:

- Be a well-known minister
- Be an author of bestselling books
- Be a wealthy entrepreneur
- Own your own business

No! Your dream could be to raise godly kids. Can you get a picture of that in your mind? Can you see your kids worshiping God? Can you see them becoming youth leaders in the youth ministry?

Your dream could be to build a dream house. See it inside. Imagine it. Build an image of that dream on the inside of you and then get it down on paper.

Your dream could be to get your house in order. It's all junked up right now, and you've just become used to living that way. But your dream is to have a clean, organized home. Get a vision of that. Get a picture of it and put it on paper. Keep that vision before you.

Your dream could be to go back to school and get your degree. See the degree with your name on it: "Bachelor of Arts degree, and your name."

Maybe you have a dream of writing and publishing a book. See yourself holding that finished product. See your name on the cover of that book. Picture people reading your book and their lives being changed because of it. Picture yourself signing that publishing contract. Picture yourself signing books at an author appearance! Write the vision down. Picture it.

I'm telling you, I have done these things, and it works!

You Have to See It First!

I recently heard a story about an animal called the African Impala (I thought it was a car). They can jump 10 feet high and up to 30 feet in length. However, you will see them held behind a four-foot wall at the zoo. Why? Because the Impala can't see over the wall, he will not even attempt to jump where he can't see first! He has to *see* where's he's headed before he will jump!

I believe that is an example to us: We need to see where we're headed first. You need to picture your dreams and goals! Just like it took time to develop the blueprints for our house, it takes time with the Lord to discover His next step for your life. Time with God is not about a clock; it's about consistently meeting with Him.

What Do You See Yourself Doing?

God said to Abraham, recorded in Genesis 13:14: "Lift your eyes now and look *from* the place where you are" (*NKJV*, emphasis added). In other words, get a vision of where you want to be. Stop looking at where you are and look at where you want to be!

Genesis 13:17 says, "Arise, walk in the land" (*NKJV*). Two guidelines: You've got to see something and you've got to be willing to go after it!

We read about the Lord speaking to Jeremiah and how He wanted Jeremiah to see what He saw:

Then the word of the LORD came to me saying: "Before I formed you in the womb *I knew you;* before you were born

I sanctified you; I ordained you a prophet to the nations."

Then I said, "Ah, Lord GOD! Behold, I cannot speak, for I am a youth."

But the LORD said to me: "Do not say, 'I am a youth,' for you shall go to all to whom I send you, and whatever I command you, you shall speak. Do not be afraid of their faces, for I am with you to deliver you," says the LORD.

Then the LORD put forth His hand and touched my mouth, and the LORD said to me: "Behold, I have put My words in your mouth. See, I have this day set you over the nations and over the kingdoms, to root out and to pull down, to destroy and to throw down, to build and to plant."

Moreover the word of the LORD came to me, saying, "Jeremiah, what do you *see*?" And I said, "I see a branch of an almond tree."

Then the LORD said to me, *"You have seen well, for I am watching over my word to perform it."*

And the word of the LORD came to me the second time, saying, "What do you *see*?" And I said, "I see a boiling pot, and it is facing away from the north" (Jer. 1:4-13, *NKJV*, emphasis added).

What if Jeremiah had said, "I don't see anything"? The truth is there was no life anywhere. All the trees were gone. Everything was dead. It was cold. Nothing was green anywhere. Nevertheless, Jeremiah saw new life, activity, alertness and growth. He saw change!

See by Faith!

I'm asking you today: *What do you see by faith?* What do you see your-self doing? What do you see God doing in your life? God wants you to see something inside. He wants you to see a BIGGER PICTURE than where you are today!

Whatever you see, write it down! No matter how foolish it looks right now or how crazy other people will think you are, write it down! God wants you to dream big! He doesn't want you to stay where you are another year. You should be able to look back next year at this time and say, "Wow! Look what God has done in my life in one year's time!"

I recently read an article about Professor Dave Kohl at Virginia Tech who did a study on successful people and goal-setting.[1] He found that people who *wrote their goals* earned nine times as much as those who didn't. Why? They had a vision. They had something in front of them that kept them focused on achieving the goal.

This professor asked people, "What are your goals for life?" Eighty percent said they didn't know. Sixteen percent said they had goals but had never written them down. Four percent said that they had goals written down but they had never gone back to look at them. Only 1 percent said they had written goals and they reviewed their goals on a weekly basis. He went on to say, "Do you know who those 1 percent are?" Millionaires!

The road to success for these millionaires were:

1. They had goals.
2. They wrote their goals.
3. They reviewed their goals consistently.

If it's a new house you're believing God for, get a picture of that house. Put it on paper. Carry it around with you. Stay focused on it. Sow seed toward your dream.

If it's a new car you're believing God for, get a picture of that car. Write the price down. Carry that dream around with you. Look at it consistently. Sow seed toward it. Believe God for it.

If the dream is owning your own restaurant, or starting your own day-care business, or writing your own books, then picture your dreams on paper.

I actually have a notebook of dreams that I look at every single day. I've got magazine clippings in there of things I'm believing God for. I've even got checks written out that I'm believing to give to the Lord one day! I've got my dreams on paper and I review them consistently; and I am watching God bring them to pass one by one.

God is no respecter of persons. He will do the same thing for you if you'll prepare for your dreams now! Remember, He said, "When I know you're ready, get ready!"

They say the average person who retires dies within three years of retirement.[2] Why? No vision. They stopped seeing something to work toward! When Helen Keller was asked what could be worse than having no sight, she said, "To have sight but no vision."

I want your dreams to be so much bigger than your memories of the past. I want you to be convinced that your life is not over! There are places you need to see . . . statues you need to climb . . . cities you need to tour . . . books you need to read . . . people you need to meet . . . pictures you need to take. Dreams you need to pursue!

Live life to the fullest! It all starts with making your relationship with God your top priority. He will cause you to dream bigger than you ever have before. And He expects you to write those dreams down, picture them and start pursuing them.

The apostle Paul said, "One thing I do [it is my one aspiration]: *forgetting what lies behind* and *straining forward* to what lies ahead, I *press on* toward the goal to win the [supreme and heavenly] prize to which God in Christ Jesus is calling us upward" (Phil. 3:13-14, *AMP,* emphasis added). The *King James Version* says, "I press toward the mark." "Pressing on" means "I'm determined!"

I heard someone say, "It's not where you start, but *whether* you start." In other words, you may have a dream of writing books and publishing them all over the world. If that's your dream, then what have you written? Have you written a chapter yet? Are you still waiting for that perfect time to *start* writing? Do you have a bunch of ideas but you haven't actually written any of them down? Desires are not enough. We have to put action behind our ideas. Start today, even if it's 10 minutes of preparing. Be ready when the publisher calls! More than that, be ready when God says, "It's time!"

Proverbs 6:6,9-11 tells us, "You lazy fool, look at an ant. Watch it closely; let it teach you a thing or two. So how long are you going to laze around doing nothing? How long before you get out of bed? A nap here, a nap there, a day off here, a day off there, sit back, take it easy—do you know what comes next? Just this: You can look forward to a dirt-poor life, poverty your permanent house guest!" (*THE MESSAGE*) Ouch! That's from the Bible!

Read what English theater director Bronson James Albery (1881–1971) wrote as an epitaph for himself:

> He slept beneath the moon
> He basked beneath the sun
> He lived a life of going-to-do
> And died with nothing done.

Don't let that be the comment at your funeral!

Persevere

Successfully walking in your calling will not be easy! If it were easy, everyone would live his or her dreams! If you claim that you are just waiting on God, remember that He is not behind you; He is in front of you. God is waiting on you. Just because a door is closed, don't assume it must be God closing the door. I like what author and professional speaker Peter Daniels says: "Kick it open!"

I've heard Peter Daniels tell a story of a man who wanted a loan for his dream. He went to one bank and was turned down. He went to another bank and was turned down. He went to another bank and was turned down. Peter's friend went to 98 banks before someone believed in his dream. Now he's made over a billion dollars as a result of persevering in his dream.

How many of us, after being denied a loan by only four banks (let alone 98), would have given up, saying, "It must not be God's plan for my life! I guess I missed it!" Satan will not roll over and play dead because you have a dream. He will do everything he can to stop you from dreaming. Anyone you see who is successful in God has had to fight to get there. In Thomas Edison's words, "Many of life's failures are people who did not realize how close they were to success when they gave up."

First Corinthians 16:9 tells us, "For a great door and effectual is opened unto me, and there are many adversaries" (*KJV*). You can walk through doors of opportunity through your perseverance. You must believe in your dream and go for it against all odds.

Prophesy Your Future

As I've said throughout this book, your mouth is the most powerful weapon you have. Whatever comes out of your mouth has an influence on how your future turns out. "Death and life are in the power of the tongue" (Prov. 18:21, *AMP*). You need to begin prophesying your future because the words of your mouth have everything to do with what happens in your life.

When my sister and I were little girls, we would sit on the front porch swing and play games with our little dog, Candace Olivia Marie Savelle the First. We called her Candy for short! We would cry out in excited and happy voices, "Candy, come here, girl," and she would start running toward us. Before she got to us, we would change the tone of our voices and say, "Candy, you better stop. Stop right there." And she would put her little brakes on. Then we would say to her in high-pitched voices, "Come on, girl, you can do it!" And her tail would wag and she'd come running. We did this over and over. Candy would walk forward, then back up; walk forward, then back up. Consequently, she got nowhere but confused.

I can't help but think that's exactly what we do in our own lives with the words of our mouths. Just as Candy stopped or went forward in response to our words, so are your circumstances connected to what you say. You can't speak faith-filled positive confessions over your life one day and then the next day talk about what a failure you are. You have to get your mouth in line with your dreams.

Remember that anything God wants you to do will be impossible. It will require your speaking positive words over your life in order for it to happen. I've heard many ministers say, "Some things will not happen in your life until you begin speaking them out!"

I highly encourage you to make a list of things you are believing to happen in your life and begin speaking them out daily! I began doing this awhile back, and I cannot even tell you how many things on my list have happened. Believe me, it works! You are fighting your past with a plan this way!

Do It *Now*

Procrastination is the enemy of success. You can be your own worst enemy by procrastinating on pursuing your calling. Evangelist Dwight L. Moody was once asked which people gave him the most trouble. His response was, "I have had more trouble with Dwight L. Moody than any other man."

Some people tend to think there's a perfect time to do everything. There isn't. So they wait. And wait. And wait some more. If you wait for the perfect timing, you'll wait forever. And the more you wait, the more tired you'll get.

Nothing can be determined for you. This is your life, your destiny and your calling that must be answered by you now.

DO IT NOW!

Don't wait for the first day of the month to write your obituary. Do it now.

Don't wait for your birthday to start the workout plan. Do it now.

Don't wait for two more semesters before you take that class. Do it now.

Don't wait until you *feel* like getting out of that ungodly relationship. Do it now.

I'm talking about your future. When you get inspired to do something, especially if you feel something stirring in your spirit, saying, "Get with it already," then you need to do something about it within 24 hours or the odds are against your ever acting on it.

I recently discovered that one of the biggest hindrances to success is knowing what to do but not actually doing it. It has been reported that three hours after you attend a seminar, you only remember 50 percent of what you learned. Twenty-four hours later, you only remember 50 percent of that! One month later, you have less than 5 percent recall of what you heard.[3]

You could finish this last little bit of the book, close it up, put it on a shelf and not refer to it ever again. I could knock on your door 30 days from now, and you'd say, "Terri who?"

Your past is behind you; your future is ahead of you. Don't let another year go by waiting, wandering, wasting. Jesus said, "No man, having put his hand to the plough, and looking back, is fit for the kingdom of God" (Luke 9:62, *KJV*). Receive the blood of Jesus that can wash your entire past away. Reach out and take hold of the clipboard that's being handed to you with your name boldly written across the top. Start taking one step at a time toward your destiny.

My prayer for you today is that your dreams will reach further and be greater than any memories of your past. You are headed for a wonderful future. You are headed for a life beyond your wildest dreams. It's time to start moving!

Notes

1. David M. Kohl and Barbara J. Newton, "Questions Generation X Is Asking About Finance and Investments," *Farm Business Management Update*, December 1999. http://sites.ext.vt.edu/newsletter-archive/fmu/1999-12/genX.html.

2. Suzanne G. Haynes, PhD, Anthony J. McMichael, MD, PhD, and Herman A. Tyroler, MD, "Survival After Early and Normal Retirement," *Journal of Gerontology*, 1978, 33(2): 239-278. http://geronj.oxfordjournals.org/cgi/content/abstract/33/2/269.

3. D. A. Sousa *How the Brain Learns* (Reston, VA: The National Association of Secondary School Principals, 1995).

CHAPTER CHALLENGES

WHEN YOU LOOK BACK . . . *YOU'VE LOST YOUR FUTURE*

Write Your Own Obituary

_____

YOUR FULL NAME

_____

YOUR BIRTH DATE

_____

_____

_____

_____

_____

_____

_____

_____

_____

_____

_____

_____

_____

CHAPTER 2

WHEN PAIN BRINGS YOU TO YOUR KNEES . . . *YOU CAN BE HEALED THERE*

1. Schedule time to be alone with God. I mean it. Think of it as seriously as if you were scheduling time to be with someone you greatly admire and respect. You wouldn't cancel on him or her. You wouldn't just not show up. You wouldn't forget about it. You wouldn't consider grocery shopping more important. You would be committed to the appointed time to meet. Don't prioritize your schedule; schedule your priorities. Being alone with God is the biggest priority of your life. It affects your entire destiny. And make sure nobody is around. You need the house to yourself.

   When am I going to spend time alone with God? Fill out the Time Map on page 213.

2. Worship God from your heart. Note that this is not a formula or a method to get God to make changes in your circumstances. Worship is a condition of the heart, and God knows the intent of your heart. He is more interested in your heart than your performance. Worship Him by bowing down at times and offering a physical surrender of complete and total dependence on Him. Magnify His names and His attributes out loud.

Time Map

	Sun	Mon	Tues	Wed	Thurs	Fri	Sat
5 AM							
6 AM							
7 AM							
8 AM							
9 AM							
10 AM							
11 AM							
12 PM							
1 PM							
2 PM							
3 PM							
4 PM							
5 PM							
6 PM							
7 PM							
8 PM							
9 PM							
10 PM							
11 PM							

3. Practice listening for God's voice. Take a journal with you and write down anything that comes up in your spirit. Read it over and over to recharge your spirit. Journaling your times with the Lord will build your confidence in your ability to hear from Him. "Thus speaks the LORD God of Israel, saying: 'Write in a book for yourself all the words that I have spoken to you'"(Jer. 30:2, *NKJV*).

4. Find one or two songs and make yourself sing them out loud during your worship time alone. Who cares if you feel foolish? It's warfare, and it works!

5. Use the name of Jesus over every distraction and every attack of Satan in your life. Declare it out of your mouth and say it with power in your voice! Send Satan away screaming!

6. Consistency is the key to change. I can't say it enough. Give God time to reveal Himself to you. You can change a bad habit or cultivate a good habit in 21 days. Make a commitment to meet with God, and have integrity with yourself.

CHAPTER 3

WHEN YOU ADMIT IT'S BEHIND YOU . . . *YOU'RE FREE TO MOVE FORWARD*

1. Continue your goal of spending alone time with God. Plan it on your calendar and don't let anything interrupt your plan.

2. On the next few pages, I encourage you to make a list of every horrible thing you've done that seems to still be haunting you. If you can think it, it's still there. Write it down. Don't write with the fear of anyone reading this. This is a time between you and God. He already knows everything anyway. It's time to give your past a burial so you can move into the new things God has for you. Take your time and begin writing one by one those memories that are still ever present in your thought life. Regrets, hurts, wounds, scars—get them out of your mind and on paper.

3. Next, write down every hurt or injustice that you feel someone else has caused in your life. Put down the date that it happened (or the year), the person's name and write what he or she did. You may find that you need a few days to do this. When I did this, I had no idea how many pages I would fill up of the things I was still holding onto. Write everything down, even if it hurts. Even if you were mad at God, write about it.

4. Hold up these pages before God and confess it all as sin. Ask God to forgive you for those sins. He doesn't need to read them to know what you did. He knows. It's you that needed to get it all out. Ask Him to cleanse you from all unrighteousness. Now believe that His Word is the Truth and you are 100 percent forgiven. Then present your hurts to the Lord and, going down the list, declare with your mouth that you forgive by faith everyone who has hurt you in the name of Jesus.

5. Here's the best part. Rip these pages out the book! After you have confessed the sin and chosen to forgive those who have hurt you, tear the words into little shreds of paper that could never be put back together again! Do not leave one word legible. Tear that paper up as if you are ripping it out of your heart never to be remembered again. Now thank the Lord out loud for loving you and giving you a fresh start.

Date

Memory of My Past

Date	Person to Forgive
————	_____
————	_____
————	_____
————	_____
————	_____
————	_____
————	_____
————	_____
————	_____
————	_____
————	_____
————	_____
————	_____
————	_____
————	_____
————	_____
————	_____
————	_____
————	_____
————	_____
————	_____
————	_____

CHAPTER 4

WHEN YOU HAVE A PLAN . . . *YOU WON'T LOOK BACK*

Men decide their habits; their habits decide their future.
The secret of your future is hidden in your daily *routine.*

Take the time to write down what you want to pursue in your daily life. As you sit quietly and meditate on these things, keep the above two quotes in the back of your mind. The areas of your life you need to work on don't have to be the same ones I chose. They should be whatever is most important to you.

When you write down your list, take some time and answer the four questions for each area. Use these answers to guide you toward putting your plan into action.

My Faith Goals (My Relationship with God)

1. What am I going to do?

_____

_____

_____

_____

2. Why am I doing this?

_____

_____

_____

_____

_____

3. How am I going to do this?

_____

_____

_____

_____

4. When am I going to do this?

_____

_____

_____

_____

My Family Goals (My Home Atmosphere and Family Relationships)

1. What am I going to do?

_____

_____

_____

_____

2. Why am I doing this?

_____

_____

_____

_____

3. How am I going to do this?

_____

_____

_____

_____

_____

4. When am I going to do this?

_____

_____

_____

_____

My Fitness Goals

1. What am I going to do?

_____

_____

_____

_____

_____

2. Why am I doing this?

_____

_____

_____

_____

_____

3. How am I going to do this?

_____

_____

_____

_____

_____

4. When am I going to do this?

_____

_____

_____

_____

My Financial Goals:

1. What am I going to do?

_____

_____

_____

_____

_____

2. Why am I doing this?

_____

_____

_____

_____

_____

3. How am I going to do this?

_____

_____

_____

_____

4. When am I going to do this?

_____

_____

_____

_____

_____

My Friendship Goals

1. What am I going to do?

_____

_____

_____

_____

_____

2. Why am I doing this?

_____

_____

_____

_____

_____

3. How am I going to do this?

_____

_____

_____

_____

_____

_____

4. When am I going to do this?

_____

_____

_____

_____

My Free-time Goals:

1. What am I going to do?

_____

_____

_____

_____

2. Why am I doing this?

_____

_____

_____

_____

3. How am I going to do this?

_____

_____

_____

_____

_____

4. When am I going to do this?

_____

_____

_____

_____

_____

CHAPTER 5

WHEN THE MEMORIES WON'T GO AWAY . . . *YOU HAVE TO GET AGGRESSIVE*

Check each step as you do it.

1. Make a list of 10 things you have to be thankful for. Make yourself give thanks to the Lord by reading this list out loud as many times as you can today. Do it every single day this week.

1. _____

2. _____

3. _____

4. _____

5. _____

6. _____

7. _____

8. _____

9. _____

10. _____

2. Choose a time and place to be alone with God to do nothing but give Him praise. Release all that heaviness off of you by shouting, jumping, running and simply losing yourself in praise to God. Don't be concerned about how foolish you may look; be determined to be free! Praise Him for who you need

Him to be in your life: your Healer, your Deliverer, your Provider, the Restorer of your soul, your Savior, your Prince of Peace, your Hiding Place, your Strong Tower.

3. Speak the Word of God every opportunity you have. Use the Scriptures listed on the following page and speak them out loud, out of your mouth. Do it often. Do it daily. Memorize them. Prophesy your future and Satan's defeat. Speak them continually until they are actually happening in your life. You can do it!

Scriptures to Read Out Loud

"He restores my soul" (Ps. 23:3, *NKJV*).

"Casting down arguments and every high thing that exalts itself against the knowledge of God, bringing every thought into captivity to the obedience of Christ" (2 Cor. 10:5, *NKJV*).

"Let the words of my mouth and the meditation of my heart be acceptable in Your sight, O Lord, my strength and my Redeemer" (Ps. 19:14, *NKJV*).

"Many are the afflictions of the righteous, but the Lord delivers him out of them all" (Ps. 34:19, *NKJV*).

"May your unfailing love be my comfort" (Ps. 119:76, *NIV*).

"My grace is sufficient for you, for My strength is made perfect in weakness" (2 Cor. 12:9, *NKJV*).

"In my anguish I cried to the Lord, and he answered by setting me free" (Ps. 118:5, *NIV*).

"The righteous cry out, and the Lord hears them; he delivers them from all their troubles. The Lord is close to the brokenhearted and saves those who are crushed in spirit" (Ps. 34:17-18, *NIV*).

"I sought the Lord, and He heard me, and delivered me from all my fears" (Ps. 34:4, *NKJV*).

"Fear not, for I am with you; be not dismayed, for I am your God. I will strengthen you, Yes, I will help you, I will uphold you with My righteous right hand" (Isa. 41:10, *NKJV*).

CHAPTER 6

WHEN YOU'RE TEMPTED TO GO BACK . . . *YOU COULD BE FALLING INTO A TRAP*

Check each step as you do it.

1. Know your weaknesses. Make a list of the top 10 areas where you are easily tempted to go backward. In what areas have you fallen in the past? Be honest with yourself.

   1. _____

   2. _____

   3. _____

   4. _____

   5. _____

   6. _____

   7. _____

   8. _____

   9. _____

   10. _____

   Look over your list. Are most of your temptations pretty much the same?

2. What lures you away from God? Is it a person? If so, who?

   _____

   _____

_____

_____

Is it several people? If so, who?

_____

_____

_____

Is it a substance? If so, what?

_____

_____

Is it something immoral? Is there a place you shouldn't go? Which one? Name it.

_____

_____

_____

Guard yourself against this temptation by realizing ahead of time that it is a trap!

3. Obey God. As bad as it hurts, choose to do what God is telling you to do. What is God telling you to do? Think about it and write it down.

_____

_____

_____

4. Be honest with yourself. If God Himself showed up in front of you right this minute, what do you think He would want removed from your life? Write it down.

_____

_____

_____

Remember: Partial obedience is still disobedience, and disobedience opens your life up to a curse. Endure the pain that your flesh will feel while it is suffering, knowing that the pain won't last forever. It's only temporary.

5. Write down statements, quotes, sayings or anything else you hear this week that speak to your situation. Write them down in one place and read them once a week. If you're discouraged, take them out and read them again. Let them speak to your life situation.

_____

_____

_____

_____

_____

_____

_____

_____

CHAPTER 7

WHEN THE SOUL TIES ARE PAINFUL ... *YOUR PAIN WON'T LAST FOREVER*

Check each step as you do it.

1. Make the decision for yourself that you want to please God more than any other person. Get alone with God and tell Him that. Even though your feelings may not support you, and you may be questioning why you don't "feel" like obeying God, keep in mind that your spirit and your flesh are continually at war with each other. It's normal. Just press in to God and conform your will to His.

2. Continue your daily habit (or start now) of hearing the Word of God every single day. Read it or listen to it on CD or on your iPod. Do not let a day go by without filling your Spirit with the Truth even if it's 10 minutes. Only the Truth will set you free.

3. Wean yourself from any ungodly soul tie. Do what you need to do to resist the overwhelming temptation to stay in that relationship. Fight your fears with a plan. Have a plan for when the phone rings. Have a plan when the weekend comes. Have a plan when your emails are piling up. Do not give in to Satan's traps to keep you bound.

Who do you need to let go of?

_____

4. Clean out your house. Set aside a time to go through your house room by room and clean out any reminders that have painful memories or negative emotional attachments to your soul. It won't be easy, but once you do it, it's over and you can move forward. What needs to be removed from your surroundings?

_____

_____

_____

_____

5. Break the power of your words. Get alone with God and bring those vows, promises and commitments before Him, taking authority over their power to keep you bound. Simply pray this prayer:

Father, in the name of Jesus, I come before You with praise and thanksgiving for being my loving Father. Thank You for pouring Your love on me, for forgiving me for sinning against You and for having such mercy on my life. I lift every ungodly word spoken out of my mouth to You, and I break the power of those words in Jesus' name. I am no longer bound by ungodly soul ties to _____, and I am no longer snared by the words of my mouth. Every ungodly promise, vow and commitment no longer has control in my life. I bind you, Satan, in Jesus' name. You have lost your power and your authority in my life. You may have affected my past, but you will not hinder my future. I curse you, and I render you powerless in my life in the magnificent name of Jesus. I am free from wrong soul ties!

CHAPTER 8

WHEN YOU LET GO OF YOUR PAST . . . *YOUR CALLING WILL BE CALLING*

1. Close your eyes and just imagine what God sees when He looks at your life here on earth. Apply the following questions to all areas—not only to the physical, but to the spiritual as well. How will your goals and dreams, as they relate to these questions, further the kingdom of God?

What do you see yourself doing?

_____

_____

_____

_____

What do you think God created you to do?

_____

_____

_____

_____

How do you see your life 10 years from now?

_____

_____

_____

What do you want to do right now if money, age, and education were no factor?

_____

_____

_____

_____

Who do you want to reach?

_____

_____

_____

What kind of influence do you want to have?

_____

_____

_____

_____

Where do you want to be living?

_____

_____

_____

What does your house look like?

_____

_____

_____

What do you see your children doing?

_____
_____
_____
_____

How do you look?

_____
_____
_____
_____

Can you see yourself at your ideal weight? What is it?

_____
_____
_____
_____

What about your finances? Can you see yourself being able to write a check for $1,000 to a ministry? What about $10,000? Can you see it?

_____
_____
_____
_____

Practice imagining your dreams.

2. Make a list of 10 things or 10 places you want to see before you die (such as the Eiffel Tower, the Lincoln Memorial in Washington D.C., the Grand Canyon, Big Ben in London, the Golden Gate Bridge in San Francisco, and so forth). Start with just 10.

1. _____
2. _____
3. _____
4. _____
5. _____
6. _____
7. _____
8. _____
9. _____
10. _____

Never stop dreaming. Never stop setting goals. Never stop living in today and pursuing your God-given destiny! Your dreams are far greater than any memories of your past.

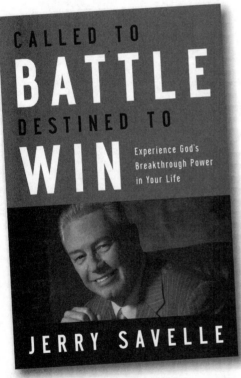